IN MY BROTHER'S SHADOW

IN MY BROTHER'S SHADOW

UWE TIMM

Translated from the German by Anthea Bell

BLOOMSBURY

First published by Verlag Kiepenheuer & Witsch, Köln, 2003 under the title
Am Beispiel Meines Bruders

First published in Great Britain in 2005

Copyright © 2003 by Verlag Kiepenheuer & Witsch, Köln

Translation copyright © Anthea Bell 2005

The moral right of the author has been asserted

Bloomsbury Publishing Plc, 38 Soho Square, London W1D 3HB

A CIP catalogue record for this book is available from the British Library

ISBN 07475 7391 3
10 9 8 7 6 5 4 3 2 1

Typeset by Palimpsest Book Production Ltd,
Polmont, Stirlingshire

Printed by Clays Ltd., St Ives plc

All papers used by Bloomsbury Publishing are natural,
recyclable products made from wood grown in well-managed forests.
The manufacturing processes conform to the environmental regulations
of the country of origin.

above the battle's fury —
clouds and trees and grass —

William Carlos Williams

Lifted up into the air – laughter, jubilation, boisterous delight – that sensation accompanies my recollection of an experience, an image, the first to make a lasting impression on me, and with it begins my self-awareness, my memory: I'm coming in from the garden, entering the kitchen where the grown-ups are gathered, my mother, my father, my sister. There they stand, looking at me. They must have said something that I don't remember, perhaps: Do you see anything? And then they glanced at the white cupboard, which I was told later was a broom cupboard. I can see hair showing above the top of the cupboard, that image impressed itself on me very distinctly, fair hair. Someone has been hiding behind the cupboard – and then he comes out, my brother, and lifts me up in the air. I can't remember his face or what he was wearing, probably his uniform, but the situation is perfectly clear in my mind: all of them looking at me, the moment when I spot the fair hair behind the cupboard, and then the feeling of being raised in the air – I'm floating.

That is my only memory of my brother, sixteen years my senior, who was severely wounded in the Ukraine at the end of September, a few months later.

30 September 1943

Dear Papi

I'm sorry to say I was badly wounded on the 19th I got a rifle shot through both legs and now they have been amputated. They took the right leg off below the knee and the left leg at the thigh I'm not in such bad pain any more please comfort Mutti soon it will all be over I'll be back in Germany in a few weeks' time and then you can visit me I wasn't taking risks.

That's all for now

Love to you and Mama, Uwe and everyone

from Kurdel

On 16 October 1943, at eight in the evening, he died in Field Hospital 623.

He accompanied me through my childhood, absent and yet present in my mother's grief, my father's doubts, the hints my parents dropped when they were talking to each other. They told stories about him, little tales of situations that were always similar, showing how brave and decent he was. Even when he wasn't the subject of discussion he was still present, more present than other dead people, in anecdotes and photographs, and in the comparisons my father drew with me, the younger son, the *afterthought*.

I have tried to write about my brother several times, but I never got beyond trying. I read his letters from the front, and the diary he kept while he was serving in Russia: a small exercise book with a pale brown cover bearing the word *Notes*.

I meant to compare my brother's entries with the wartime records of his division, the SS Death's Head Division, to find out more details that might expand on his brief references. But whenever I started reading the diary or the letters I soon had to stop again.

It was a fearful reluctance of the kind I felt as a child for a certain fairy tale, the story of *Bluebeard*. My mother used to read me the tales of the Brothers Grimm in the evenings, many of them several times over, including *Bluebeard*, but that was the only one with an ending I didn't want to hear. The moment when Bluebeard's wife tries to enter the locked room after he has gone away, in spite of his prohibition, was so sinister. When my mother came to that point I would ask her to stop reading. Only years later, when I was grown up, did I reach the end of the fairy tale.

Then she turned the key in the lock. As the door opened, a torrent of blood flowed out to meet her, and she saw dead women hanging from the walls. Some of them were only skeletons. She was so frightened that she closed the door at once, but the key jumped out of the lock and fell in the blood. She quickly picked it up and tried to wash the blood away, but in vain, for when she had wiped it off one side of the key it appeared again on the other side.

Another reason was my mother herself. While she was alive it was impossible for me to write about my brother. I already knew what she would say in answer to my questions. Let the dead rest in peace. Only when my sister,

3

the last of the family to have known him, had died too was I free to write about him, and by free I mean that I could ask all the questions I liked without having to consider anyone or anything else.

Now and then I dream of my brother. Usually these are just fragmentary dreams, a few images, situations, words. But one of them has left a precise impression on me.

Someone is trying to break into my home. A figure stands outside, dark, dirty, covered with mud. I want to close the door. The faceless figure is trying to force his way in. I brace myself against the door with all my might, forcing back the man who, faceless though he is, I know for certain is my brother. At last I manage to push the door shut and bolt it. But to my horror I am holding a rough, ragged jacket in my hands.

My brother and I.

In other dreams he has the face I know from his photographs. He wears uniform in only one of these pictures. There are many photos of my father showing him with and without his steel helmet, in a field cap, in his fatigues, in dress uniform, with a pistol, with a Luftwaffe dagger. But there is just this one picture of my brother in uniform, showing him at roll-call in the barrack square, holding his rifle. It is a distant shot of him, and so blurred that only my mother could claim to have recognised him at once.

Since I started writing about him I have had his photograph on my bookshelves. It shows him in civilian clothing, probably around the time he volunteered for the Waffen SS. His thin, smooth face is photographed slightly from below. The hint of a vertical line between his eyebrows gives him a remarkably severe expression. His fair hair is parted on the left.

A story that my mother told over and over again was of how he went to volunteer for the Waffen SS but lost his way. She told it as if what happened afterwards could have been averted. It was a story I heard so early and so often that I see it all as if I had been there too.

In December 1942, late in the afternoon of an unusually cold day, he went out to Ochsenzoll, where the SS had their barracks. Snow had settled on the roads. There were no signposts, and he had lost his way in the gathering dusk, but he went on past the last houses towards the barracks. He had noted their position on the map. Not a soul in sight, and he sets out into open country. The sky is cloudless, with a wispy mist only above the hollows in the ground and the stream-beds. The moon has just risen above a spinney. My brother is about to turn back when he sees a man. A dark figure standing by the roadside, looking across the snow-covered field and up at the moon.

My brother hesitates for a moment, because the man stands there as if frozen, and does not move even though he must have heard the footsteps coming closer, crunching through the snow. My brother asks if he knows the way to the SS barracks. For a long time the man stands motionless, as if he hadn't heard, but then he turns slowly and says: There. The moon is laughing. And when my brother again asks the way to the barracks the man tells him to follow and sets off at once, walking fast, striding vigorously; on he goes through the night without stopping, not once turning round. It is far too late to arrive at the recruiting centre now. My brother asks the way to the railway station, but the man goes on without replying, past dark farmhouses, past cowsheds with cattle lowing hoarsely inside. The ice in the cartwheel ruts splinters underfoot. After a while my brother asks if they are going the right way. The man stops, turns and says: Yes, we're going to the moon, there, look, the moon is laughing, laughing because the dead lie so still.

That night, when he came home, my brother told them how he had been afraid for a moment, and that later, when he had found his way to the railway station, he met two policemen looking for a madman who had escaped from the Alsterdorf asylum.

And then?

Next day he set off early in the morning, he found the barracks and the recruiting centre, and he was accepted at once: height 6 feet, hair fair, eyes blue. So he became a sapper in the SS Death's Head Division. He was eighteen years old.

His was considered one of the elite units among the SS divisions, along with the Reich Division and the

Leibstandarte Adolf Hitler Division. The Death's Head Division had been recruited in 1939 from the guards of Dachau concentration camp. As a special distinction, its men wore the death's head badge not just on their caps, like the other SS units, but on their lapels too.

A strange thing about the boy was the way he would disappear from time to time in the apartment. Not because he feared some punishment; he simply disappeared for no obvious reason. All of a sudden no one could find him. Then, equally abruptly, he would reappear. Our mother always asked where he had been hiding, but he wouldn't say.

At this time he was physically very weak. Dr Morthorst had diagnosed anaemia and a heart flutter, and nothing would induce my brother to play out of doors. He would not leave home, or the shop to which a flight of stairs gave access, or the workshop that our father called an *atelier*. He would disappear somewhere in our small apartment, which consisted of four rooms, kitchen, lavatory and storage room. Mother, having just left the room, would come back a little later. He wasn't there. She called for him, looked under the table, in the cupboard. No trace. He might have vanished into thin air. This was his secret, the only really odd thing about the boy.

Later, many years later, my mother told me how, when the windows of the apartment were being painted, she discovered the boxed-in wooden structure like a window seat – we lived on the ground floor. This wooden structure could be moved, and behind it lay catapults, a torch, exercise books and some books about wild animals: lions, tigers, antelopes. My mother couldn't remember the other titles. He must have gone in there to read, listening to his parents' footsteps and voices while he himself was invisible.

By the time our mother found the hiding-place my brother had joined the army, and when he came home on leave she forgot to ask him about it.

Apparently he was a pale child, positively transparent, so he could disappear, suddenly appear again, and be found sitting at the table as if nothing had happened. Asked where he had been hiding, he simply said underground, which was not entirely untrue. It was strange conduct, but our mother asked no more questions and did not spy on him, nor did she tell our father.

He was rather a timid boy, said our mother.

He didn't tell lies. He was well-behaved, and above all he was brave, said our father, brave even as a child. People described him as *that brave boy*, even distant relations. These were word-for-word statements of fact, and he will have taken them that way himself. The entries in his diary begin in spring 1943, on 14 February, and they end on 6 August in the same year, six weeks before he was wounded, ten weeks before his death. Not a day goes by without an entry. Then, suddenly, the diary breaks off. Why? What happened on 7 August? After that there is just one entry, undated, but I shall come to it later.

8

14 February
We expect action any time now. On the alert from nine-thirty.

15 February
Danger over, waiting.

And so it goes on, day after day. The word *waiting* recurs, and then *same old routine* or *parading for roll-call*.

25 February
We move to rising ground to attack. The Russians retreat. Night, taxi-way under fire.

26 February
Baptism of fire. Russians beaten back to strength of 1 battalion. In position at night with machine gun, no winter clothing.

27 February
Combing the terrain. Plenty of loot! Then on again as usual.

28 February
1 day's rest, big louse hunt, on to Onelda.

This was one of those passages where I would stop, hesitating to read on. Couldn't louse hunt mean not just delousing a uniform, but something very different? On the other hand, if so he would not have said *1 day's rest*. But then, that *Plenty of loot!*

What exactly do the words conceal? Armaments? Why the exclamation mark, which is otherwise rare in his notes?

14 March
Airplanes. Ivans attacking. My looted Fahr machine gun, too heavy, shoots like a mad thing I can hardly hold it steady, a couple of hits

15 March
Making for Kharkov ahead of small remnant of Russians.

16 March
In Kharkov

17 March
Quiet day

18 March
Constant bombardment by Russians 1 bomb in our quarters 3 wnded my Fahr MG not working I take my MG 42 and fire at 40 H (?) sustained firing

And so it goes on, brief entries in pencil, in irregular handwriting, maybe written on a truck, in his quarters, before the next operation, day after day: *weapons inspection, rain and slush, MG sniper practice, drill, flame-thrower 42.*

21 March
Donez
Bridgehead on the Donez. 75 m away Ivan smoking cigarettes, fodder for my MG.

This was the place where, when I came upon it earlier – and it positively leaped out at me from the top left-hand side of the page – I read no more, but closed the notebook. It was only with my decision to write about my brother, and thus about myself too, to unleash memory, that I felt free to look closely at what he had recorded there.

Fodder for my MG: a Russian soldier, perhaps his own age. A young man who had just lit a cigarette – drawing on it for the first time, breathing out, relishing the smoke rising from the burning cigarette before drawing on it again. What was he thinking about? The troops who would soon arrive to relieve them? Tea, a piece of bread, his girlfriend, his mother, his father? A small cloud of smoke dispersing in that landscape, a place drenched in moisture, remnants of snow, melt-water lying where it had collected in the trenches, the tender green of the willow trees. What will he have been thinking, the Russian, the Ivan, at that moment? *Fodder for my MG*.

For quite a long time he was a sickly child. He ran high temperatures that no one could explain. Scarlet fever. A photograph shows him in bed, his fair hair tousled. Our mother says that in spite of the pain he was astonishingly composed, a patient child. A child who spent a great deal of time with his father. Photographs show the father with his son: on his lap, on his motorbike, in the car. Our sister, two years older than my brother, is ignored as she stands beside them.

The pet names he gave himself as a child: Daddum, Kurdelbumbum.

My father thought that I, the afterthought, spent too much time with women. When he was serving with the Luftwaffe stationed at Frankfurt an der Oder, my father wrote in a letter to my brother in Russia: *Uwe is a nice little thing but a bit spoilt, ah well, once we're back home again all that will sort itself out.*

I was what they used to call a *mummy's boy*. I liked the scent of women, that mixture of soap and perfume, I liked and sought – an early sensation, this – the softness of breasts and thighs. Whereas he, my big brother, was always devoted to our father, even as a small child. And then there was our sister, two years older than my brother, eighteen years older than me, who got little attention and hardly any affection from our father, so that she developed a rather brittle, aloof manner which our father in his own turn described as sullen, and which only put yet more distance between them.

Karl-Heinz, my father's big boy, why did it have to be him? My father would fall silent, and you could feel the loss in him, you could see him wondering which of us might better have been spared.

My brother was the boy who told no lies, who was always upright, shed no tears, was brave and obedient. A fine example.

My brother and I.

Writing about my brother means writing about my father too. My likeness to him can be seen in my likeness to my brother. To get close to them in writing is an attempt to resolve what I had merely held on to in my memory, to find myself again.

They both go on journeys with me. When I come to borders and have to fill in entry permits, I enter my father and brother too, as part of my name, writing them in block capitals in the appropriate box: Uwe Hans Heinz.

My brother was keen to be my godfather, to add his name to my own, and my father wanted me to have his name, Hans, as well. He wanted to live on in someone else, at least in name, for by 1940 it was already clear that the war was not going to be over very soon, and death became more and more probable. Asked why my brother had volunteered for the SS, my mother offered several obvious reasons. *Out of idealism. He didn't want to be left out. He didn't want to shirk his duty.* She, like my father, drew a clear distinction between the SS and the Waffen SS. By now, after the end of the war and when those terrible pictures had been shown, films of the liberation of the concentration camps, people knew what had gone on. *Bastards*, they called the SS, *criminals*. But the boy was with the Waffen SS. *The SS was just a normal fighting unit. The criminals were the others, the Sicherheitsdienst, the intelligence and security service. The task force groups. Especially the men at the top, the leaders. Abusing a boy's idealism.*

First a 'Pimpf' – a 'little squirt' – then a member of the Hitler Youth. Marching to the sound of trumpets,

13

battle games, singing, a uniform with metal tags. But unlike you, said my mother, your brother never wanted to play with soldiers.

I was against it, she said, I was against Karl-Heinz volunteering for the SS.

And what about my father?

My father, born in November 1899, had volunteered in the First World War and joined the field artillery. The odd thing is that I know almost nothing about his life at this time, just that he was a cadet and wanted to be an officer, but once the war was lost that was out of the question, so like thousands of other men demobbed from the army he joined a Freikorps volunteer unit and fought the Bolsheviks in the Baltic. But exactly where, for how long, and why I don't know. And since almost all his documents and letters were burnt when our apartment building was bombed in 1943, there is no way of finding out now.

A few photographs in an album show my father during this period. One of them, dated 1919, is of a group of young men in uniform. Some are wearing boots, others gaiters. They are sitting on a broad flight of stone steps that may be part of a monument. He and another young man are lounging on their sides in front of their seated companions, a popular pose for group photographs at the time. His left arm rests on the ground and he is laughing: a fair-haired, good-looking young man. The young soldiers, clean-shaven, their hair carefully parted, could be students and probably were. One of them wears rings on both his little finger and ring finger, another has a signet ring. They sit there casually, laughing. It looks as if my father, lounging in front of them, has just cracked a joke. Other photographs also show him with comrades, snapshots from a soldier's life. In one he is standing on a camp bed that has just collapsed. There he is in a night-shirt, his uniform cap tipped rakishly over his left ear. A soldier's life is the life for me, tralala, tralala, tralalee. Straw-thatched cottages, peasants in Russian smocks, soldiers eating, a horse-drawn cart festooned with steel helmets, those rather large German helmets of the First World War with two air-holes shaped like warts at the sides. It was a life relished by many youths of eighteen or nineteen: adventure, comradeship, fresh air, liquor and women, and above all no regular work – the photos make that clear.

When people ask what my father did, I can give no single answer: he was a taxidermist, a soldier, a furrier.

He liked to tell me stories when I was a child, he took his time over it, explained the world to me. He used the historical paintings in circulation on the cigarette cards of the time to illustrate his tales: Old Fritz, Frederick the Great, sitting under the bridge and holding his greyhound's muzzle shut as the enemy hussars ride by; the Prussian general Friedrich Wilhelm Seydlitz at the battle of Rossbach throwing his clay pipe in the air as the signal to attack; the body of Charles XII of Sweden carried from the field of battle by his officers. Rumour had it that one of his own men shot him. My father had a very good knowledge of history, and most important of all, he could tell a lively story. But by the time I might have begun asking questions about his tales we were at odds. An obdurate and increasingly bitter struggle between us began when I was sixteen. He was narrow-minded, opinionated and strict, while I preserved a stubborn silence in the face of his odious regulation of everyday life: no jeans, no jazz, home by ten in the evening. Everything was either forbidden or compulsory and subject to rules: a system of rules that made no sense to me and was obviously inconsistent. It was not just that I began to look at him critically now that I was older; our circumstances had changed too. He was no longer the man he had been in the early 1950s, when he was doing really well, when he had *made it*, between 1951 and 1954. Those were the three or four years of his life when what he wanted to be matched what he actually was. The economic miracle was in full swing at home. He had made it, he had finally made it. He had furnished the apartment, he had a fine sea-green car, a four-door Adler, the 1939 model with the first ever gear change to be mounted on a steering column. There were so few such cars in Hamburg at this time that the traffic police standing in their white coats at the Dammtor saluted as he drove past. At Christmas he gave them presents of packs of cigarettes which my mother had wrapped in gold paper, tying them up with a silver bow and adding a little sprig of fir. He drove round town to the road junctions where policemen stood on little platforms directing the traffic, and stopped briefly beside each officer to hand him the package. *Happy Christmas.* In return the policemen waved him through the road junctions all the year round, briefly touching the peaks of their caps.

My father liked to receive a military salute. He once came on leave from the front to Coburg, where my mother and I had been evacuated, and took me with him to his barracks. My mother had sewn silver epaulettes on to my coat. Just before we reached the barracks he told me to go first. The sentries presented arms and grinned. I learned to click my heels and make a little bow. It was an amusing sight, so friends and relations told me later when I was grown up; I had clicked my heels briskly, in just the right way.

So that was me: a five-year-old in a little grey coat, clicking his heels and bowing. The smell of sweaty leather: that was my father. A strange man in uniform lying in my mother's bed one day: that is my first memory of him. His high boots stand on the floor, their leather tops turned over. On the bedside table – a very clear memory – lies a pistol fastened to a belt. I saw him lying there with his mouth open, snoring. He was on leave. If I sniff my watch strap I can once again catch that smell of sweaty leather, and he, my father, is closer to me than in any of my pictorial memories.

Then one day the grown-ups talked earnestly to me, told me to stop doing a trick I'd only just learned: I mustn't click my heels. And whatever you do, don't say Heil Hitler, understand? They spoke to the child in soft and urgent tones.

It was 23 April 1945, and American soldiers had moved into the city.

★

17

Who taught me to click my heels? Not my mother, with whom I was living in Coburg at the time. She had a profound aversion to anything military – drill, war games, the war itself – and not just since her son's death. Yet the images, the uniforms, held a certain fascination for her. But she can't have taught me to click my heels. It was probably my father, visiting us on leave, or the other military men, the Nazi functionaries who went in and out of Frau Schmidt's house, where we were staying. Frau Schmidt was widow of the chairman of the local district council.

If the Russians come, said Frau Schmidt, I shall get myself a rope.

My brother's letter to my father of 11 August 1943:

If only we could finish Russia off quickly. We need ten times as many SS divisions as we have now. I think that would do for the Russians, but we won't manage it this year.

Everything is still the same here, I'm in good health, I have enough to eat, but I'm worried about everyone at home, we hear reports of air raids by the English every day. If only they'd stop that filthy business. It's not war, it's the murder of women and children – it's inhumane. I hope to hear from you and Mutti soon, but tell Mutti not to send any more parcels, it would be a pity for anything to get lost and I have enough. Let our dear little Uwe eat the things instead. Now, dear Papi, best regards and very good wishes –

Your comrade Karl-Heinz

★

There are no photos showing hanged Russians or the shooting of civilians, just *everyday* scenes showing ruined buildings, streets, towns, such as are found in my father's album too. Do they show Kharkov? My brother took part in the recapture of Kharkov in 1943. Even if we assume that he did not participate in the murder by the SS of civilians, women and children, because he was serving with a tank unit, he must have seen civilian victims, the starving and the homeless, people exiled, frozen and killed in the course of the war. He does not mention them; presumably their suffering, all the destruction and the killing, seemed to him normal and thus *humane*.

General Heinrici, commander of a corps in the central sector in 1941, writes in a letter to his wife:

You feel the destructive violence of war only when you think of details or individual human fates. I expect books will be written about this later. The populations of towns have disappeared almost without trace. The only people left in the villages are women, children and the old. All the others have been uprooted and are drifting around the expanses of Russia. According to accounts by prisoners, they huddle together on railway stations, a human conglomeration, begging the soldiers for a crust of bread. I believe the number of victims claimed by the war from among these displaced people who die of illness or over-exhaustion is as great as the number lost in bloodshed.

One of General Heinrici's diary entries:

I tell Beutelsbacher not to hang partisans only 100 metres from my window. Not a pleasant sight in the morning.

Gryasnovo, 23 November 1941
After the situation report, a memorial service for our fallen, for this is Remembrance Day [. . .] Then a walk to the 'dead Russian'. An unusual destination for a stroll; there's a Russian who has been lying frozen in the snow for weeks. I must get the locals to bury him.

My mother was an old woman of seventy-four when she went on a bus trip to Russia with a party of tourists, to Leningrad by way of East Germany, Poland and White Russia, and then back from Leningrad via Finland and Sweden. She nurtured the entirely baseless hope that she might be able to make a detour to visit my brother's grave, or at least some place close to it. That was her wish, to visit his grave just once. The Heroes' Cemetery of Snamyenka in the Ukraine. The number of his grave was L 302.

The boy longed fervently for boots – lace-up, calf-length boots. He didn't enjoy being in the Hitler Youth. He had to do punishment drill several times. His troop leader made him crawl down the street among the pedestrians. He didn't mention it at home until a family friend saw him one day and told his father, who complained to a Hitler Youth regional leader. There was no more punishment drill for my brother after that.

He was dreamy as a child and adolescent, absent-minded, and sometimes, so my mother told me, he just disappeared as if some ghostly hand had led him away. He said little, you didn't know what was going on inside his head. He was good. A good child, she said. A quiet child. Dreamy. But she said the same of me too, and perhaps from her point of view she was right. My silence preserved her image of me as a good boy. My parents thought I was at the youth group meetings of a Hamburg stamp-collecting club when in fact I was roaming the streets of Sankt Pauli, which despite being named after St Paul is a distinctly unsanctified part of the city of Hamburg, with its casinos, bars and brothels. It was the opposite of my world at home, the quiet, tidy apartment where sex was hardly ever mentioned, at least certainly not in front of me. I walked down Talstrasse and saw the women standing in the entrances of buildings, the drunken sailors, I saw the striptease joints, the bars, the public houses, a bar called the Silbersack where, as my father put it, the *dregs of humanity* met: smugglers, black marketeers, drug addicts, gamblers, ladies of easy virtue. I was very keen to meet the dregs of humanity. The noise, the laughter, the shrill mirth of the women – all the sounds I heard emanating from the Silbersack were alluring, so near but yet so far. Once, when I loitered by the door rather too long, the doorman came out and said: move on, sonny, off you go. The glimpses you might catch: women sometimes holding their coats open when a man came by, with nothing on beneath them but underwear, silk stockings and suspenders.

He mentions no dreams in his diary, no wishes, no secrets. Did my brother have a girlfriend? Had he ever made love to a woman? Did he know the sensation of having another body close to yours, urgently close, feeling your own body in it, feeling yourself in it, through it, experiencing your own sense of dissolving in that other body?

The diary is devoted exclusively to the war, to preparing to kill, to the perfection of methods of killing with flame-throwers, mines, target practice. Once he mentions a variety show, once a dramatic performance, once a film that he must have seen in a cinema at the front. *24 April. Bridge-building – our tanks are on the way. 30 April. Movie. The Great Shadow.*

He doesn't comment on it. Did he like the film?

Cheated of his own story, of a chance to experience his own feelings, he was reduced to putting a brave face on things.

The little cardboard box sent on to my mother after his death contains the photo of a film actress, Hannelore Schroth. A round, gentle face, brown eyes, dark brown hair, full lips with dimples on each cheek.

The Great Shadow.

9 October 1943
My dear Mutsch
I've already written to tell Papa I'm badly wounded
Now I'm writing to you too, to tell you they've amputated both my legs.

My handwriting will surprise you but it's the best I can do lying in this position.

You mustn't think they amputated my legs right up to my buttocks. The right leg was taken off 15 cm below the knee and the left leg 8 cm above the knee
The pain is not too bad or I wouldn't be writing to you.
Dear Mutsch [don't] cry now be brave I'll be able to get about on my artificial legs just the same as before and anyway the war's over for me and you'll have your son back even if I'm badly injured
It will probably be a few weeks before I come back to Germany I'm not fit to be transported yet
So again, dear Mutsch, don't grieve for me and don't cry that will just make life difficult for me.
Love to Hanne and Uwe
don't tell Uwe about it when I come home with my artificial legs in 1 or 2 [illegible] *[he'll] think I always had them.*
Love from your
Kurdelbumbum

This is written in pencil in distorted, sometimes very large handwriting, probably under the influence of morphine. He was wounded by the River Dnieper on 19 September 1943. He must have lain there all night, his shattered legs roughly bandaged for him by his comrades.

That night my mother had dreamed of a parcel that came by post. When she opened it, it contained bandages, and when she unwrapped them, those long, long white strips of bandaging, a bunch of violets fell out.

★

She really did have that dream on the night he was wounded. Full of anxiety, she had told friends and relations about it. The telegram with the news of his injuries did not arrive until days later – at almost the same time as the news of his death.

Apart from small, everyday rituals, not meant entirely seriously – but still, you never know – like spitting on a coin you have found, or knocking on wood three times, she disliked any kind of superstition and extravagant fantasising. But when she spoke of this dream she would say that there are more things in heaven and earth than are known of in our philosophy. She drew her own conclusions: she wouldn't brood on it any more, nor would she bother anyone else with it. But she was sure there was a wordless form of communication reaching beyond the limitations of space and time.

Dear Frau Timm,

The following items of property belonging to your son, SS Sturmmann Karl-Heinz Timm, who fell on 16 October 1943, have arrived here:

10 photographs
1 comb
1 tube of toothpaste
1packet of tobacco
1 notebook
1 Verw.-Abz. [Wounded Medal], *black*
1 notice of award of the E.K. II [Iron Cross Class II]
1 certificate of authorisation to hold the Wounded Medal, black
1 telegram

Letters and notepaper, various
These items are enclosed for you.
Heil Hitler!

Signed [illegible]
SS-Obersturmführer (F)

The files, the reports and the books of the time are full of abbreviations, unintelligible and mysterious sets of letters, usually capitals, both concealing and revealing the bureaucratic threat of the hierarchical system.

The rank of Obersturmführer was equivalent to first lieutenant, but what does that (F) mean?

My mother kept my brother's letters, decorations and diary in the little cardboard box. It lay in her dressing-table drawer for fifty years. She used a soap called *Nonchalance*, and always kept several bars of it in the same drawer, with her eau de toilette and perfume. It had an unmistakable scent which lasted longer than any physical part of her. The scent still clings faintly to that box and the diary.

I have sorted out the letters that my brother wrote to our mother and father and have put them in envelopes, giving them labels. *The letter with the pressed pinks. The letter about the machine gun.*

There were certain stories they always told about my brother: the boy who gave his stamp collection away one day. He didn't even swap it for anything, my father proudly said. The boy who had a pet lizard. The boy who was too dreamy to do very well at school. The story of how once, as a very small child, he jumped off the five-metre board at the swimming pool. He climbed the ladder and simply jumped. Bravo, cried his father, who had told him: go on, just climb up there and jump. The boy who was so good at rounders. The boy who was found to have a heart flutter and went to Bad Nauheim for treatment at the spa. There he is in the picture with another boy of his own size and age. They must have been about twelve or thirteen. They stand there with their arms round one another's shoulders, their faces turned to look at each other, relaxed and smiling slightly. The other boy's name was Heinrich, and my mother said they were best friends.

He himself, his life, emerges only from his diary and the few letters that have been preserved. This is the *recorded* memory of him.

His favourite food was mashed potato with fried eggs and spinach. Our mother would drip melted butter into the runny yolk. He liked Brussels sprouts. When he was ill he used to ask for rice pudding with sugar and cinnamon.

He didn't drink, didn't smoke. Until he reached the front. He sent his cigarettes to our father, but now he was drinking, carousing all night, then there was roll-call in the morning. *Drill with a splitting head.* That way, they said, the lads were *knocked into shape.*

★

The diary says nothing about prisoners. Nowhere does he write about taking prisoners. Either the Russians were killed at once or they did not surrender. A third possibility is that he didn't think it worth mentioning.

75 m away Ivan smoking cigarettes, fodder for my MG.

Heinrich Himmler, addressing men of the Waffen SS in Stettin on 13 July 1941, three weeks after the invasion of the Soviet Union:

We are involved in a conflict of ideologies and races. In this conflict National Socialism, an ideology based on the value of our Germanic, Nordic blood, stands on the one side, stands for a world as we envisage it – good, decent, socially just, perhaps still blemished by isolated flaws, but on the whole a happy, beautiful world, full of culture, the world our land of Germany represents. On the other side stands a nation numbering 180 million, a mixture of races and peoples even whose names are unpronounceable, and whose nature allows them to be shot down without mercy or compunction.

Did his unit, the 4th Armoured Engineers Battalion of the Death's Head Division, take part in what were described as mopping-up operations? Mopping up partisans, civilians, Jews?

Bombed out, and the boy fell soon afterwards. That was the blow Fate had dealt our family, that was war. *Everything destroyed.*

A letter to Karl-Heinz from his father:

Frankfurt an der Oder, 6 August 1943
  My dear Karl-Heinz
  I came back from Hamburg today after weekend leave – a weekend leave extended to almost 14 days, because while I was there 4 air raids totally destroyed Hamburg, our beautiful city. At least 80% of it lies in rubble and ashes. I came home with Mutti from the railway station at 1 in the morning and at about quarter past there was an air-raid warning, and when I heard enemy aircraft coming in for a big raid I shouted to everyone still in bed to get down to the air-raid shelter in the cellar, and hardly 20 minutes after that a high-explosive bomb fell on the building. The Tommies scattered phosphorus everywhere and the whole place burned. All that's left of our building is a few ruined walls.

My father, who happened to be back on leave from the front, and my sister, then twenty years old, had snatched up a few things as the upper floor of the three-storey building was already burning: an occasional table, a chair, a suitcase from the lumber room, a few towels, a duvet, two porcelain figurines, a porcelain plate and a small box which my sister thought might hold valuables, but which in fact contained the Christmas tree decorations.

They had grabbed these things from wherever they happened to be; beams and parts of walls were already crashing down. They carried them out into the street where all the other tenants of the building stood, including my mother with me, her little boy, in her arms.

The buildings all around them were on fire.

The rest of what I know is anecdotal: how my sister tried to save some bed linen and was pushed aside by my father as a beam fell. How the window panes on the second floor of the apartment building exploded in the heat, one by one. How a rain of ashes fell from the sky, casting a dark pall over everything. The ash contained everything people had saved for and bought over the years – and now it was falling, a dirty grey, on their hair, on their blouses. 25 July 1943; it had been a hot summer day.

Another clear picture, and my own memory begins here: huge torches to the right and left of the street. Burning trees.

And this picture too: little flames floating in the air.

The danger of smoothing it all out in the telling. *Speak, Memory*. Only from today's perspective do we see the chains of cause and effect ordering things, enabling us to understand them. A picture: the child I am then, aged three, has been put in a pram, covered with wet towels, and is being wheeled along Osterstrasse.

It was not until later, when people talked about them, that the little flames floating in the air were explained: scraps of net curtains torn from the burning buildings by the firestorm.

Years after the war the tales of these events, tales which accompanied me through my childhood, were told over and over again, gradually taking the edge off the original horror, making what had happened intelligible and finally entertaining: how my sister and my father first dumped our belongings in the middle of the street, then put the child, me, in the pram and covered me up with towels soaked at a burst water main, how my parents and sister, leaving the few things they had saved just where they were in the street, hurried down Osterstrasse in the direction of Schulweg, burning buildings to their right and left – the right-hand side of the street was burning particularly fiercely – on to Lastrupsweg, more burning buildings, how they took refuge in the crowded air-raid shelter where people were sitting with strange composure, how my father reported to a Luftwaffe staff unit that very night, and was found at the home of relatives after two more days of air raids, unshaven, suffering from lack of sleep, in his dirty white summer uniform. And the tales he and others told us: bodies, discovered clutching water pipes in the cellars of burnt-out buildings, that fell to dust at the first draught of air. Some people had run outside, were caught by the firestorm and swept into the burning part of town; others, their clothes on fire, had jumped into the canals. But the phosphorus burnt on the water too.

The air-raid shelter into which my mother had run with my sister and me was at the corner of Schulweg, in Israel's Leather Goods store. The shop is still in existence today. My mother told me that in 1938 there were large notices in the windows: *Please Note! The name notwithstanding, the proprietor of this store is pure Aryan! Signed: Israel, Leather Goods.*

Another of my early memories: the people in the air-raid shelter. An old man weeping. A woman with a birdcage on her lap, a bird hopping excitedly back and forth. Another bird lying on its back at the bottom of the cage, as if it had just fallen off its little swing.

Letter from my brother to our father:

17 August 1943
Your letter came this morning. I just can't take it in. To think that 80% of Hamburg is in ruins, we've become hardened soldiers here, but I still had tears in my eyes. It was home, our home, a place of happy memories and now that irreplaceable treasure is gone, simply isn't there any more, is destroyed.

No Jews were allowed in the air-raid shelter.

I once saw an air-raid shelter, a bunker, on top of which a family home had been built after the war. Friends of ours bought it. Going down into it was like a return to childhood, the damp, oppressive, tunnel-like, labyrinthine atmosphere, since the bunker was divided up by partitions. Rusty ventilation pipes ran along the walls. There were notices: No Smoking, Gas Tap. It was a peculiar descent, and conjured up long-forgotten images. The surprising thing was that when the lights were turned off the white walls still looked bright. Even sixty years after the war those walls glowed with phosphorus paint. Only slowly and very gradually did their light dim.

The two Biedermeier porcelain figures saved from the burning building by my father and sister are slightly damaged. One of them, a shepherdess with a basket of flowers on her arm, has a hand missing. The other is a little group: two seated women in Biedermeier period dresses are listening to a man who stands reading aloud to them, a book in his left hand, his right hand raised to emphasise a point. The book was knocked out of his hand, and the fingers of his right hand are missing too. After the war these disabled figures stood on the bookcase, memorials to what our parents had lost in the war.

But the Christmas tree baubles that my sister brought out of the burning building just before it collapsed suffered no damage at all, a fact that was mentioned again and again as a curiosity.

It was strange, the way in which shock, alarm, horror gradually became comprehensible through repeated telling, the way experiences slowly faded when put into words: *Hamburg in rubble and ashes. The city a sea of flames. The firestorm.*

In the late autumn of 1943 my mother and I were evacuated to Coburg to live with relations.

My brother had trained as a furrier. That was what he wanted to be, said my mother, and the diary confirms it.

It contains several drawings showing, among other images and sketched with touching clumsiness, a design for the window display of a furrier's shop.

The astonishing thing was that he obviously liked the trade. Unlike me, for I too trained in it and passed my qualifying exam, but I had only one idea in my head, and that was to do something else: to write, to read. Even then I had a passion for reading and writing, and under no circumstances did I want to take over my father's furrier's business. It bored me, once I had learned all about it: how to make coats of Persian lamb, mink, coypu and beaver, design their cut and make the pattern. I learned it all so well that I passed the qualifying exam with distinction. My father disliked the shop too, seeing it as a necessary evil. But it made him independent. Independence mattered. Independence was the last remnant of a sense of superiority. He also hated the trade, and was not entirely master of it; it had come his way by accident. He had found a sewing machine for making up furs on a bombed site. But the discovery was not just coincidence; his pre-war work as a taxidermist must surely have directed his attention to that sewing machine. It was a time when many such items had been displaced and, torn from their familiar context, lay abandoned in the ruins.

The ruined buildings contained copper and lead pipes, metals that would fetch a good price later at a second-hand shop, as well as pots and pans, stoves, heaters, lathes and tools, sometimes bizarrely fused together. And stranded vehicles stood in the streets down which the German armies had retreated: Wehrmacht trucks riddled with bullets, field kitchens and ostentatious artillery, abandoned cars from which any undamaged parts had been removed. All these were channelled into the barter economy where they found their own value; it was a form of barter that followed the laws of supply and demand, if necessary adjusting to the approximate currency represented by American cigarettes.

What did my father want to be?

Wishes and disinclinations such as these, particularly those never expressed, reach far and wide and, like the lines of a magnetic field, determine our actions.

What did my father want to be? Not a furrier, anyway, and still less a taxidermist.

What was his real ambition?

After his time in the Freikorps, he had lived in a number of different cities. He studied zoology, although he had never taken his final school exam. I now wonder how that came about, or did he simply tell us a fictional, invented biography? He had lived for a while in Stuttgart, where he evidently went hungry, surviving on carrots for weeks on end until he collapsed from undernourishment. His sister Grete, who had visited him in Stuttgart, told us this story. He was close to the Organisation Consul, or even a member of it. So his sister Grete said.

The November Criminals, who concluded the armistice of November 1918. The *Dolchstoss*, the 'stab in the back' –, Social Democrats and Jews at home were said to have betrayed the German army in World War One. System time.

The Organisation Consul was the Freikorps kangaroo court, and was responsible for the murder of Reich Foreign Minister Walther Rathenau in 1922 and Reich Finance Minister Matthias Erzberger in 1921, both alleged by the extreme right to be traitors to the Fatherland.

Once an old First World War comrade of my father's came to visit, and unusually my father talked to him alone in another room. A tall man, pale, thin-faced, with a purple scar slanting down over nose and forehead. His bushy eyebrows had grown together. The cavalry captain, my father called him, without mentioning his name. My mother didn't know it either.

In 1921 my father and an emigré Tsarist officer had tried setting up a toy factory. They had little wooden horses made by war invalids and the unemployed. He thought up advertising slogans, only one of which I can remember now: *For your pretty little dears, to make them laugh and shed no tears.*

It was at this time that he met my mother, the daughter of a hat maker with a flourishing hat factory and a shop, owner of a small villa in Tornquiststrasse in Hamburg-Eimsbüttel.

It was love, she said, not exactly at first sight but very soon after they had met a few times. There were one or two weeks between each of those meetings. She liked him, tall and slim in his *litevka*, a uniform jacket that he wore without any military insignia. He is wearing it in several photographs. If he'd been a conman he could easily have passed for a Prussian prince. One photo shows him at a carnival party in hussar's costume. He almost always has a cigarette in his hand, sometimes between his lips, at the side of his mouth in a pose you see today only on old movie posters, giving a casual little smile, his hands in the side pockets of the *litevka*. Otherwise he had no other jacket or coat, only this uniform jacket under which he wore a darned grey sweater in winter. He was a poor man with distinguished manners. He asked the hat maker for his daughter's hand, and though my grandfather had hoped for a prosperous son-in-law he gave his consent. Soon after that the young man went bankrupt over the toy factory, which can't have been very large. The Tsarist officer fled to Paris to escape his creditors; the young man was baled out by his father-in-law.

My mother said that he was the only man in the world for her.

Not that she didn't see the discrepancy between the part he played and the man he really was. But he always enjoyed credit wherever he went, although often it might not be entirely secured, and in most cases he could not cover it. If he had taken his final school examination, if he had gone on to further education, he might have been a lawyer, intelligent and eloquent as he was, or an architect, a profession in which he could surely have succeeded – he was a gifted draughtsman with a precise feeling for space – and then he would have been sure of leading a prosperous, middle-class life. As it was, he only appeared to be distinguished, while he had to work in a trade that he secretly despised.

My mother saw this weakness and tried to compensate for it without ever showing him up in company, not even by means of a wry smile or a lift of her eyebrows. She never spoke of him in derogatory terms, even when I complained about him, and there was a time, shortly before his death, when I could not speak to him without losing my temper.

She stood by him unhesitatingly. My husband, she often said, just that: my husband, and to me she referred to him as Father.

Getting married was something final, something dependable, a bond that was indissoluble once you had entered into it.

They never quarrelled in front of me. There must have been reason enough for quarrels, since my mother had a clear idea of what was realistic, of what could be done in practice. She thought little of outward appearances – she did not let them dazzle her and was personally unpretentious – and she cannot have failed to see that he was living above his means. There were discussions. She told him her opinion, calmly and firmly, but they did not quarrel in front of me. What I do remember is an admonitory: *But you can't, Hans. It simply will not do.*

The idea that parents could get divorced, and there were three or four children with divorced parents in my class at school, or even that they could live apart from each other, was unthinkable to me. Parents belonged together, irrevocably. Even after his death, when she was fifty-six years old, she said: he was the one man in the world I wanted, and I had him. However hard I try, I cannot remember any loud or violent altercations, any sulks, reproachful silences or cutting remarks from either of them. Their division of roles was too clear for that. He was in charge of economic matters, and decided which way the family 'marched'. She ran the household, helped in the shop, advised customers, lent a hand in the workshop now and then lining coats, and she looked after the child, me, the *latecomer*, the *afterthought*.

The word emancipation meant nothing to her. What would I be emancipating myself from? she asked a woman who had been one of the founders of a women's group in 1969, and came to have her fur coat altered. The coat was shockingly dirty, my mother told me later, and on top of that the woman wanted to haggle over the price of repairing it. I can't live on fine words, my mother had said, adding: I work, and I want to be paid. So that was that, said my mother, and then I held the door open for her. When she was roused she seemed to me taller than she really was.

Politics interested her only in so far as wanting herself and her family to be left in peace. She said there must never be a war again. She voted in elections, but always with the comment: they'll do as they like anyway. She voted for left-wing parties, probably partly for my sake. She was *fed up to the teeth with right-wingers*, she said, *what a bunch of rogues*.

She went to the opera, to the theatre, to museums, and

read what I recommended to her. But nothing she read or heard or saw changed her in any way. She did it simply because it was *nice* to go to the opera or the theatre now and then, and part of that was *getting dressed up*, drinking a glass of Sekt in the interval and being able to talk about her evening out the next day. She was not an intellectual. When we came to visit at Christmas or on birthdays, all of us, the children, Dagmar and I, fell on the celebrity magazines that she saved for us.

She took life as it came. She adjusted to the poverty of conditions after 1945, and lived inexpensively when *business was good*. And her ambitions? They were all for the boy, for me. The boy was to have a good life some day. What about herself? She wanted to be without financial worries. To travel. She wanted the business to do well. Her hands hurt, and so did her eyes. She didn't complain, but I saw her dabbing her eyes with a cotton-wool ball dipped in camomile tea. She had cataracts, and feared that one day she wouldn't be able to sew any more, wouldn't be able to see.

She gave up the shop when she was eighty-two. Until then she had worked there every day, keeping the accounts, selling furs, doing fittings, lining coats. She hadn't trained; she had learned the trade as she went along. Her upbringing suggested that everything should have been very different for her. A girl from a good family. But she didn't complain of her fate.

When I came to visit in those last years, when she was running the shop with just my sister and *business was bad*, so bad that she had to dip into her savings, I would find her sitting in the bright little workshop behind the show-room, lining a fur coat. I have a clear picture in my memory of her sitting there and sewing. There is a birch tree outside the window, its light green branches brushing the pane.

In the afternoon my sister would go out to buy Danish pastries or buttered almond cake, while my mother put on the kettle and laid the table: plates, cups and saucers. Then they'd sit there drinking coffee and *having a nice time*. At home in the evening they would talk about the trips my mother might like to take. And she really did begin to travel, having never left Germany until she was sixty; she went on coach trips to France, Italy, England, Russia. When she got home she stuck her photographs into albums and wrote captions under them. While she was away she sent postcards to friends, relations, me. Back at home she wrote letters almost daily. I often imagine rereading these letters some day, hundreds of them, when I can't concentrate on my work. I think they would cheer me.

My mother was thirty-eight when I was born. *A great big baby*, she said, weighing over 11 lbs. She was small and slight, only 5 feet, 3 inches tall. It was very unusual then for a woman to have a baby so late. She said she felt slightly embarrassed when her pregnancy began to show. But there was never any doubt in her mind that she would bear the child. Or in my father's mind, she said.

Their first child was born in 1922, a home birth, and it was not the son they wanted but a girl. My father probably didn't even hide his disappointment. He wanted sons, sons to make up for what had gone wrong in his own life. Sons promised more security, economic security included. His grandfather had been a farmer in Langenhorn. *Timmweg*, the place was called. He sold his land to house-building associations and spent most of the proceeds on drink and women. So did my father's own father, who had simply gone off with *a person*. All pictures of him, my grandfather, were destroyed in an act of iconoclasm. No one talked about him. He was to be forgotten. Punishment by obliteration from memory and mention.

My father, said my mother, had wanted a boy so much that he would have nothing to do with *that girl*. It was different with the son born two years later, Karl-Heinz. And indeed none of the photographs show my father in physical contact with my sister, she is never in his arms, or holding hands, or on his lap. Later, when she was in hospital and could speak only with difficulty, she said our father – she always spoke to me of 'our father', 'our mother', as if to link us personally and not just grammatically – *our father always rejected me. Unlike Karl-Heinz. He was very much a father to Karl-Heinz*. My sister lived in Karl-Heinz's shadow. Even our mother, usually so affectionate and evenhanded, paid very little attention to her wishes. My sister was like our mother, but darker; as a child her hair was almost black, her eyes dark brown.

Looks like a real little gypsy, a neighbour had said when she was small. Our mother was indignant, and never spoke to the man again.

And what about the afterthought? Mid-blond, with his father's figure, resembling him in the shape of his head too, his hairline, his profusion of hair, his hands, but with his mother's brown eyes – that was me.

My sister was called Hanne Lore, written as two separate names instead of the more common Hannelore, she insisted on that, as if this particular spelling of her name proved her unique. She hadn't developed any decisive qualities of her own that would have let her pursue her own ambitions. After school she took a domestic science course, was called up for wartime labour service, and almost drowned. A leader pushed her into a swimming pool at the deep end. The woman intended it as a drastic method of teaching someone to swim – after all, there was a war on. My sister screamed, swallowed water, sank, came up again, and sank back to the bottom of the pool. A pool attendant rescued her.

I'm one of those people who just have no luck in life, she said. She didn't make much fuss about it, just mentioned it tersely, the fact that she had *no luck in life*. Her first fiancé fell fighting with the infantry in Russia. She met another man, they got engaged, and he was taken prisoner by the Russians in 1944. She waited seven years, until 1951, and then news came that her fiancé had died in a Russian camp. She fell in love with a man who resembled our father, tall, fair, good-looking, a man who had rented a jeweller's shop; she became his best customer until our father threw him out of the house. She went on seeing him in secret and gave members of the family presents

42

of silver cutlery, spoons, forks, knives, the knives tied with a ribbon bow so that they wouldn't cut friendship apart. The man, our father discovered, had two fiancées already. That didn't deter her; she allowed him, brilliant salesman that he was, to spin her a yarn explaining why he hadn't yet broken off his two other engagements.

Such foolishness, said our father.

But she wasn't stupid, only blinded by infatuation. She didn't want to see the man as he was, only to feel, feel her own emotions, affection and tenderness, to be taken seriously, even if the man was professionally motivated by the sale of jewellery and silver cutlery. It was one of those everyday passions which express protest, rejection, contradiction all at once. The child followed the events with amazement, and it was all far wilder, more dramatic and more radical than any comparable situation would be today, for society still had much stricter ideas of what was *done* and *not done*. It was not done for a woman to run after a man.

In fact my sister's conduct was scandalous – and in the same part of town too, for the jeweller's shop was only a street away from us. It was an embarrassment for my father: his daughter going around with a man who everyone knew had two other girlfriends already.

Finally, although she was now thirty-two years old, my father forbade her to have any contact with the man. There were scenes between father and daughter: shouting, yelling, sobbing, door-slamming, bellowing.

She left home and went to be nanny and household help in a doctor's family. After two years she came back.

By now the jeweller had married another woman whose father owned a fish cannery.

My sister came back to our father's workshop to make up furs, as she was trained to do. After our father's death she met a Persian Jew whose family ran a carpet business. A kindly man who courted her for years, but she wouldn't marry him. She liked him, but in a distant way, keeping him at arm's length. She went to the cinema with him, now and then to see an operetta, and on Sundays, when the sun shone, they travelled into the city centre for lunch, went for a walk, visited a café, and he would bring her home late in the afternoon. So the years passed by.

For her birthday and Christmas he gave her gold coins, large and small, with the portrait of the Shah on them, and he gave her presents of oriental embroideries and brass plates and jugs – my mother thought it dreadful stuff. The man's name was Ephraim, and he showed old-fashioned courtesy to both my sister and my mother, indeed respect.

Once my sister went to a synagogue service with him, and once she visited his family.

When I asked why she didn't move in with the man she said: I don't like him enough to live with him.

One November morning my sister read a newspaper report about a storm over Hamburg the night before, when there had been a high tide and road accidents. *In Osterstrasse (Eimsbüttel) a car driven by 50-year-old Hekmat H. from New York was in collision with a taxi driven by Detlef*

L. (31) from Norderstedt. The American's passenger, 62-year-old Ibrahim H. of Eimsbüttel, died of severe injuries at the scene of the accident.

I found the newspaper cutting in the little case, a child's suitcase, where she kept her personal documents, a few letters, an engagement announcement, death notices and some photographs, including one of her fiancé whom I never met.

It could all have been different, she said, but quite early on she saw no way of putting things right. She lived like this until she fell sick and had to have an operation. She had just had her sixty-eighth birthday. They gave her a colostomy. At first she was full of shame and anxiety and didn't want to travel. Then, after a few months, she came to visit us and managed to crack jokes about it in front of the children when she audibly broke wind at table. Dear me, she said, one doesn't do that kind of thing. I can't go away except with that little *bottle thing*. When she came out of the lavatory she would be carrying a small bag wrapped in paper, looking slightly embarrassed on her way out to the rubbish bin.

Once, when we were alone, she wept and said: oh, it's horrible.

I travelled from Berlin to Hamburg. I sat in the dining car and looked out at the landscape I knew so well, meadows, hedges and ditches, little woods, storks in a marshy meadow. Solitary oak trees, black and white cows, brick houses, the Sachsenwald, the first bungalows, with blue spruce trees and carousel washing lines in the gardens, the central railway station. I went on to Eimsbüttel and the Elim hospital, where I had been born and where my mother died.

Elim, an oasis of rest.

She was in the same six-bed ward where my mother had been. The windows were open, the curtains moved gently. It was an unusually hot summer's day.

A wheeled trolley with a drip hanging from it stood by my sister's bed. The cannula was in the blue-tinged crook of her arm. My sister had grown thin, the flesh hung slack from her arms. Her hair, which she had tinted a light mid-brown, was dishevelled, revealing a good two centimetres of grey at the roots. The hospital night-dress had slipped, showing part of her breasts lying flat on her ribcage. Her mouth had fallen in like an old woman's. Later I saw her false teeth in the drawer of the bedside table.

I had been to her apartment first. She had carefully cleaned and tidied everything. The fridge was defrosted. An electricity bill due to be paid lay on the table in the corridor. She had made up the bed just as my mother used to, a bed too short for me, so that I had to sleep with my legs slightly bent.

The bill?

I paid it.

She was restless, her hand constantly stroking the bedspread.

Everything's all right at home, don't worry.

But she wanted to talk, she wanted to dwell on the past, on herself, our father, me.

What was I like as a child, I asked? So long as that question can be answered you still *are* a child.

Different.

How do you mean, different? Just different. But how? She thought, and said after a while: you saw lions in the bushes. Then you waved a stick about. Everyone laughed except Father, who went looking for the lions with you. She thought, and I could see it wasn't just talking she found difficult, but thinking, remembering. Our father was always so considerate, she said, he wouldn't have let them do this horrible operation.

But it had to be done, I said.

He wouldn't have let them, she said. He always took good care of me.

She wanted to see it that way, so I said, yes, maybe.

Karl-Heinz, who was so close to our father, was *a real boy*. He was proud of that boy. Very likely my brother was as timid a child as I was. Even today I find myself thinking: go on, take the plunge, dive in now. And the water is far, far below. And no one has ever told me how to dive, head first but still looking forward and not down, pushing off from the board instead of simply dropping. Once, on a rainy day when there was hardly anyone there, I went secretly to the open-air pool, climbed to the five-metre board and jumped. The ten-metre board still awaits me. It feels like an order: *you must be brave.* He was supposed to be brave but not reckless. Lying in hospital with his legs amputated, his command of language distorted by the morphine, he assures his parents that he hasn't been taking risks. Even there, mutilated, knowing himself disabled for ever, his youth gone, even there he was still a good, brave boy.

In a letter to our mother, my brother enclosed a second letter addressed to me. I was three at the time.

22 July 1943
Dear Uwe
Mummy wrote to me saying you want to shoot all the Russians dead and then run away with me. Well, that's no good, you know, I mean, suppose everybody did that? But I hope I'll be home soon and then I'll play with you, Uwe.
We're waiting to load up now, we're going to another part of the Eastern Front.
What do you do all day? I bet you're stuffing yourself with blackberries. Enjoy them!

What would make a child of three want to shoot all the Russians dead? It was how people talked at the time. But it could have been very indirect encouragement on my mother's part for him to desert, put into the mouth of a child to get past the censors. For it made no sense: if all Russians were shot dead there'd be no need to run away.

The Lüneburger Heide. The cemetery. Schleswig-Holstein. Bad Segeberg. Sunday afternoon. Walking round the lake. My father with his hat and his lightweight summer coat, carrying a pair of leather gloves, my mother with a light-coloured dustcoat over her outfit, cotton

48

gloves, the child in pale trousers, white knee-length socks, that was how we went walking along the shores of the lake. The memory of it paralyses me, paralyses my breathing, my thinking, a paralysis of memory. And another thing too: we often talked about *him* on those Sunday outings, or, when I say *often,* is it a great exaggeration of what really happened? Was it more a case of now and then, and do I remember it so clearly because my own existence was always called into question by these conversations, especially when they weren't addressed to me? The lives of both my parents were called into question too. What would have happened if . . .? A wholly superfluous question, although it rebounds on the questioner: how far, in the light of rational action, does he think that anything can be altered? During these discussions my mother never reproached my father. It seemed that he really had volunteered *of his own free will,* our father hadn't persuaded him to volunteer. But there was no need. His was only the tacit, wordless performance of what our father, obeying the dictates of society, wanted him to do. I myself managed to find words of my own, objections, questions and more questions. And words to express sadness and fear in telling a tale. The boy dreams and *tünt,* tells stories – *tünen,* a Low German verb meaning to lie, to spin a yarn, a word deriving, appropriately enough, from weaving. The boy I was did indeed weave together what he saw and heard, to give a meaning of their own to those things and to himself.

The frightened boy. The brave boy.

Letter to our father, 20 July 1943:

Our convoy of Tiger tanks has been in battle from 5 July until today, when the counter-attack ended. I'm sure you'll have read about its success in the newspaper. There was heavy fighting, Russ. Americ. and Engl. tanks only 50–100 m apart in some places, sometimes three abreast. We raced the T-34 in our personnel carrier until the T-34 got hit by a 3.4 or a Tiger. I'll tell you all about it later.

Don't write this to Mutti.

Greetings from your Kamrad Karl-Heinz.

The brave boy had volunteered for an elite unit. A very different elite from the one with which our father had fought in the Freikorps; those men were all that was left of the feudal aristocracy, and you could enter their circle without ever being really accepted, merely tolerated. *Semper talis*, always outstanding, was the motto of the Fusilier Guards, and my father liked to quote it. But that was what his life was not; it wasn't outstanding. That word *honour* and the way he emphasised it. *That is not honourable.*

Anyone could join the Waffen SS if his certificate of Aryan descent showed that he had no Jewish blood at least as far back as his great-grandparents. *Pure Aryan descent.* The family tree. Nobility for the whole nation. Himmler, who was still raising chickens in 1928, sought models for the SS in the Middle Ages, the castles of the Teutonic Order, games like those held at the old Scandinavian *Thing* meetings, settlement in the east. *Umvolkung*, repopulation.

A ridiculous, silly term, but deadly in real life. The chosen ones were to be defined by race, by membership of the nation and not of a social class; as in the nobility, blood was the criterion, not blue but Aryan, German blood, the master race with a vocation to rule. The Black Corps, the SS. The elite. And it was no coincidence that the leaders of the Special Action Groups in the Soviet Union – those expressly favoured by Himmler – were academics: eight were lawyers, one a university professor, and SS Standartenführer Blobel, head of Special Detachment 4a and responsible for the death of sixty thousand human beings, was an architect. To the surprise of the American officers who interrogated them, they were not primitive brutes, but men with a literary, philosophical and musical education, men who listened to Mozart, read Hölderlin – one could wish they had not. They had a keen sense of right and wrong, and consequently did everything possible to conceal what they had done. When the Red Army was marching on Kiev, the dead in the ravine of Babi Yar were exhumed by prisoners under the super-vision of the SS, the bodies were burned, and then the prisoners themselves were shot. The price of the diesel oil used to burn the bodies was recorded in the accounts. The bureaucracy of death. Otto Ohlendorf, a qualified economist, head of Special Action Group D and an expert on statistics, justified the killing of ninety thou-sand men, women and children by comparing it to the Children of Israel's annihilation of their enemies in the Bible. The master race. This was the megalomania of the petit bourgeois and even those lowest on the social scale clearly thought that it was better to guard twelve 'inferior humans' with a rifle than do any work themselves. This was the mortar that held the ideology of the master race together. The mythical attribute of German blood was enough; whether you were lazy or industrious, stupid or intelligent, you were one of the masters. The national community resembled the noblemen my father had encountered in the Baltic, who respected the purity of the family tree. And the SS, the Schutzstaffel, was the model for that community, bound together solely by the notion of blood and feeling itself an elite, superior to all other races. SS members had their blood group tattooed on their upper arms. Although this was a sensible measure enabling a man's blood group to be instantly known if he was wounded, its deeper significance was to express blood brotherhood, an ideology which constantly returned to the arguments of blood, the family tree, breeding. It was the counterpart to the numbers tattooed on the forearms of concentration camp inmates to mark their rejection from the human community. Victims and oppressors alike were defined by numbers.

And nothing, such is our deep and despairing realisation, neither education, nor culture, nor what is known as spirituality kept the perpetrators from doing their evil deeds. Conversely, as Jean Améry wrote in *At the Mind's Limits*, the same was true of the victims in the camps: culture and education brought no strength, no comfort, could not mobilise resistance, were powerless. A soft, sensitive expression hovered around the mouth of the persecutor, for instance Heydrich when he played the violin.

As for the victims, Améry aptly wrote: *Like those lines of poetry about the speechless walls and the banners flapping in the wind, philosophical statements lost their transcendent nature and we regarded them partly as objective comments, partly as idle chatter: where they meant something they appeared trivial, and where they were not trivial they no longer meant anything. We needed no semantic analysis or logical syntax to recognise this: a glance at the watchtowers, the smell of burning fat from the crematoria reaching our nostrils, was enough.*

There can be no attempt at explanation. Nothing written with a view to tracing the causes of those events, classifying or understanding them is any help; it can only be a form of self-defence against what was found. The photograph taken by Lee Miller in Dachau after the liberation of the camp by the Americans shows an SS man drowned in a stream by inmates. One can make out his face and camou-flage uniform, slightly blurred by the clear water flowing over them, as if he is emerging from menacing depths. Lee Miller captioned her photo 'The Evil'. Suppose my brother had been posted to join the concentration camp guards?

My parents never asked that question aloud. Did they think it? I imagine they must have thought it at the very least – and how great was their horror at the thought? What they did wonder and discuss out loud was what would have happened if he hadn't joined the SS. But that was not an outright rejection of the war, which would have had to come years earlier. They were simply questioning his choice of military unit; suppose he had simply joined the Wehrmacht? The Wehrmacht troops suffered fewer losses than the Waffen SS. And what's more, the Wehrmacht had nothing to do with *those terrible things*. In the 1950s and early 1960s the Wehrmacht had a reputation for *decency*. The Wehrmacht were soldiers who had *only* been doing their duty. The Waffen SS had done more than their duty. *Unsere Ehre heisst Treue*, were the words on their belt buckles, *Our Honour Means Loyalty*. If only he had joined the Afrika Korps! This idea, of course, as my parents knew, ignored the fact that a man could just as well have had both his legs shot off in Africa too. Perhaps, they thought, Fate would have decided differently in Africa.

And it was indeed my brother's wish to fight in the Afrika Korps. Rommel. The Desert Fox. Africa. A romantic notion. His diary contains a drawing of a lion leaping out from behind a tree, palm leaves, a snake on the ground. The lion is very well drawn. Another rather naive sketch shows a shop window. The wording over it says: *Furs – Animals – Skins. Garments for Ladies and Gentlemen. Animal Heads. Taxidermy. Animal Sculptures*. Then our father's name: *Hans Timm*.

Early in 1929 my father opened a taxidermy business after working for some years with a well-known Hamburg taxidermist. He had no real training, but had picked up the necessary knowledge as a boy from his uncle in Coburg. He had a good eye for movement and proportions, and an outstanding talent for stuffing animals to make them look lifelike. Photographs of the animals my father stuffed are evidence of his skill: a zebra, a lion, many dogs, and in particular a gorilla. Various photos show the process of taxidermy: my father in a white coat modelling the gorilla's body in plaster, and then the final result, the animal reaching for a tree with its left arm, mouth open to show its teeth, right arm beating its chest. You can clearly see the prehensile toes on its feet and the surprisingly small penis. The animal's eyes gleam, and so do the jaws showing its huge teeth. It is clinging to the tree, and you can't tell if it has just climbed down to attack the observer or is caught in a moment of panic, ready to run for it. An apprentice who had worked with my father told me later that this gorilla terrified all the women customers, until one lady complained of the penis and it had to be covered with an apron. From then on the gorilla invited ridicule.

One photograph shows my brother in a sailor suit, holding a school satchel. My father had the sailor suit with gilded buttons made especially for him. The boy's expression is grave. A dog is sitting beside him, a German Shepherd. Is it stuffed or alive? I think it's Bello, the German Shepherd they had at the time.

The gorilla was stuffed for an American museum; I wish I knew which one. Perhaps it is still on display some-where in a zoological department in Denver or Chicago. My father worked for collections and museums as well as private customers. His work was illustrated and praised in trade journals. At the beginning of the thirties he was offered a post in Chicago as a taxidermist at the Natural History Museum. He spent a long time wondering whether to accept the offer, which would have meant emigrating. But he decided to stay and set up a business of his own for the sake of the family. Another more profound reason was that he didn't like America, he wanted to stay in Germany. Germany was not just a country, it was *the* country, full of a history which was his own, which permeated him, and he was proud of it. It was not just his passport that was German, it was his homeland, his language, his people. In fact that is the meaning of the word *deutsch,* German, from Gothic *thiot,* meaning tribe, people.

He couldn't imagine emigrating except in dire emergency; as he saw it, the idea smacked slightly of treachery. Thomas Mann, who had spoken during a BBC talk in support of the bombing and destruction of Lübeck, was a traitor, and so was Marlene Dietrich, who had appeared in American uniform, singing along with the US Army.

After the war, in the hard winter of 1946, we received a Care parcel. It contained things unknown to me such as oatmeal, brown sugar, corned beef, dried milk and maple syrup. The parcel also contained two shirts and a pair of shoes, new black shoes with leather soles and rubber heels. Small patches of red leather were set in the heels. These shoes were admired by friends and relations as if they were a work of art. My father said at the time, and often repeated it: I'm a fool, why didn't I go to America?

He put the shoes on, but they were two sizes too small, and several attempts by the cobbler to stretch them made no difference. They were still too small. He wore them all the same, wore them all summer until they gave him corns, and only then did he part with them, bartering them on the black market for food and cigarettes and three bars of Swiss milk chocolate. I got a small piece every evening after supper. I remember the taste of it even now.

America, Sweden and Switzerland, those were the rich countries, and from them came chocolate, school meals, and biscuits. America, from my childish viewpoint, was a mighty country, much mightier than my father's Germany, and thus of course mightier than my father. My father's generation was humiliated by America. Russia, they said, was *rich in people, but bled white by the war*. America, on the other hand, was a greater, stronger land. We adopted its values and its culture. An insult to those who had set out to conquer the world, who believed they were the chosen race. Who thought highly of their honour. And now they bent to pick up cigarette ends and had to be re-educated. *Umerziehung*: re-education.

In April 1945 a barricade was built beyond the Itz bridge in Coburg and trenches were dug on the river bank. A first lieutenant was detailed to defend this barricade from the advancing Americans. It was a warm, sunny spring day.

That morning, while I was playing, I had fallen into a

trench outside our building. I sat in the damp earth as if in a grave. The blue sky above me. I must have screamed my head off until a German soldier rescued me from the hole. Soon afterwards the German soldiers were gone; they had taken their uniforms off, put civilian clothes on, and simply left their bazookas and rifles in their attics at home. An American tank slowly pushed aside the pantechnicon trailer loaded with paving stones that was supposed to bar the bridge. Soon afterwards the doorbell rang and the frightened women of the house, my mother included, opened the door. Three GIs stood outside, one of them black. So ended the Third Reich in Coburg.

It was the liberation. Liberation from soldiers smelling of leather, hobnailed boots, saying *Jawohl*, clicking heels, those army boots marching in rhythm that you heard from far away, echoing down the streets. The victors came on rubber soles, almost noiselessly. A functional jeep with a can of gasoline and a spade at the front. The windscreen could be folded back. The smell of the gasoline was different from German fuel, sweeter. Soldiers in khaki uniforms climbed casually into the jeep. And threw chewing gum, chocolate, cookies to us children. Unknown delights.

Herr Feigtmaier in his brown uniform, chairman of the local district council, still feared and respectfully saluted only two days before, now stood in the gutter sweeping the street while the jeeps drove past close by, and he had to jump up on the pavement spattered with mud.

Overnight the big people, the grown-ups, had shrunk. An observation that I shared with many of my contemporaries.

There is probably a connection between this impression and the anti-authoritarian student revolution against our parents' generation.

Columns of vehicles moved through the city: jeeps, trucks, armoured reconnaissance cars, while the captured German soldiers followed in rags and tatters. Our eagerness to welcome the victorious advance of the American way of life – with its movies, literature, music and clothes – arose from our fathers' unconditional surrender, not just in military terms but the surrender of their values and their way of life. Adults appeared ridiculous, even if a child could not yet pin down the reason why, but it was in the air: our fathers had been demoted. It was their duty to salute. The men had to take their caps or hats off to the victors, the soldiers of the British occupying power. As a child I watched adults, including women, bend to pick up the cigarette ends the GIs tossed away. Men who had only recently been saluted themselves, with a click of the heels, who had spoken in thunderous voices of command were suddenly whispering now, saying they hadn't known anything about *all that*, saying they hadn't wanted it, saying there'd been treachery at work.

My father hated American music, movies, jazz. Americanism. Our fathers had lost the power of command in public life and could exercise it only at home, within their own four walls.

At school we couldn't be taught out of the old text-books any more. A teacher called Herr Bohnert, the only one in the school who had lost his job under the Nazis for political reasons, now taught German and history, not only speaking plainly about the stupidity and criminality of the Nazis but also investigating the causes and, using examples, criticising the *zombie-like obedience* and *deranged militarism* of the Germans. My father, when I told him, got angry about the *re-education* forced upon us by the victors. But there was nothing he could do. And I, the child, sensed that his vociferous indignation merely revealed his helplessness.

Once, in occupied France, he had seen a German soldier giving a boy an apple. The boy took the apple and contemptuously threw it away. A story illustrating pride; my father told it several times.

On a train journey an American officer offered me a bar of chocolate. I wouldn't take it. The American shook his head. My father, who was with me, kept on talking about the incident later as if it were a heroic deed. Karl-Heinz, of course, would have done just the same.

A whole generation had been deprived of political, military and intellectual power, and reacted with a sense of injury, with defiance and obduracy. Later, when the Cold War began, its strength revived, but initially, in those first years after the war had been lost, that generation's claim to dominion survived only at home, in private. And it turned against the culture of its conquerors.

One of the differences between East and West Germany, between what later because the Democratic and Federal Republics, may be that the western part of the country faced accusations of collective guilt, logical enough from a democratic viewpoint. Hitler, after all, had been elected. In the eastern part of the country, on the other hand, an automatically simplified distinction was drawn between seducers and seduced, implying that the capitalists had led the workers astray. Guilt thus became a question of class founded on economic interests. Authoritarian thinking and the behavioural patterns of the authoritarian state remained unquestioned, and were even incorporated into the socialist society as positive Prussian virtues. Economic conditions had been revolutionised, although from outside, by the Red Army and the Soviet Union. No cultural revolution accompanied the economic upheaval, no revolt against the way of life of the now guilty paternal generation. No new structures within society were tried out, free and easy relationships between the sexes and an ability to criticise the power structures of the state were not encouraged. There was no freedom of opinion, no democratically based codetermination, and there were no socially independent institutions. Every private bar was regarded as an incipient hotbed of revolt. Every duplicating machine was forbidden as potentially disruptive to the system, every pocket calculator was an object of suspicion, since it might be used to falsify the ever-rising production figures. Any criticism of this development, even when it arose from a sense of solidarity, was dismissed as ideological infiltration by the West, by America, by capitalism.

The boy couldn't remember ever being encouraged by his parents, not even his mother, to show nonconformity

– to *keep out of it,* to *be careful*, yes, but not to say no, to resist, to be disobedient. Being brought up to be brave – but preferably collectively brave – led to timidity in civil life.

When my father was released from a British POW camp he went to Hamburg, and in 1946 my mother and I returned there from Coburg. He had found the fur-sewing machine among the rubble, had oiled and cleaned it, and opened a furrier's business in a cellar, where we would soon all be living. When he came back from the camp he owned nothing but his Luftwaffe uniform, dyed green. His Swiss airman's watch, as he told people again and again, had been stolen from him by a British soldier when he was taken prisoner. And there were two stories about his pigskin-lined high boots; according to one version they had been taken from him with threats of force by liberated Polish labourers at the Dammtor railway station, according to the other he´had bartered them for butter and squirrel skins. Perhaps there were two pairs of boots and he had hidden one pair at his sister's home. In one clear memory of my father I see him walking about with a stork-like gait in ordinary shoes and tight-fitting breeches. One half of the building where he had found us a cellar to live in had been demolished by an aerial mine, so that the interior wall of one room had now become an exterior wall. Ruins lay outside the cellar window, a hilly landscape of rubble where a child could play. All kinds of things could be found in these mountains of rubble:

saucepans, taps, bathtubs, iron bedsteads, knives, water pipes, overflow pipes, clocks, sewing machines, irons, rusted and sometimes melted into odd shapes by the heat.

A semi-circular scar on my forehead is the legacy of those games in the rubble landscape, which smelled of mortar and rotting wood. Sitting on the ground with an old hammer, cleaning up a brick to build a house with the boy was struck on the forehead by part of a bicycle thrown away by another child. A veil of bright red fell over both eyes, no pain at first, just surprise at all this red on his hands, his arms, his shirt, and a little later the taste of blood and iron.

My father slept on the tacking board, a wooden surface on which the pieces of skin, once sewn together, were tacked into the shape of a coat. I can't remember where my sister was at the time. Probably with relatives in Schleswig-Holstein. I slept in the only bed with my mother. Damp came into the room through the interior wall that now faced outwards, and it froze in winter to a shiny layer that, in the evening by candlelight, became a vertical fairytale landscape. We slept with our pullovers and coats on, and my father used his dyed uniform coat as a blanket. It had the letters PW in white on the back. Prisoner of war.

I see him sitting at the sewing machine stitching the squirrel skins together, smoothing the fur, which is so thin and delicate that it shades to grey in the gentle movement caused by a slight breath of air. A tedious, fiddly job, and my father was always swearing because he had sewn in some of the fur.

It was the first fur coat he had made in his life.

After two years we were able to move out of the cellar and into an apartment. It had only one room in which my father, my mother and I lived, but it could be heated and it was dry. Three years later we moved again, to an apartment above a showroom and workshop. My father had the showroom renovated, with stained beech panelling on the walls and two large mirrors for fitting sessions. He had engaged two furriers and six seamstresses. The master furrier, Herr Kotte, had only one eye. He had been a tank driver, and a splinter from a shell had passed through the peephole and hit him in the eye. Kotte was not a good furrier, and there were often faults in the coats he made. The skins were not sewn level with each other, and the colour and length of the fur did not always match.

He doesn't see well with just the one eye, said my father. There were complaints, but he kept the war-wounded furrier on. Now and then Herr Kotte turned to face the wall, and we knew he was taking his glass eye out to wipe it with his handkerchief.

When there was a party at our place – and a great many parties were given in those days – a young man with a small furrier's business of his own was brought round. This man had had both legs shot away. Colleagues drove him to us by car, and my father carried him into the workshop, where a table had been laid on a large tacking board: cured pork spare ribs and sausages with potato salad. The man, whose legs had been amputated directly below his trunk, was put on a chair. Now and then my father carried him out to the lavatory. There was a lot of laughter, and this man laughed too, was able to laugh loud and heartily. It amazed me as a child to see him sitting there with his hands on the tacking board and laughing, positively shaking with laughter. And when they had all gone my father carried the man, who was only a torso, out to the waiting car again.

After that my mother and father sat on at the large tacking board full of empty plates, bottles and glasses, smoking in silence. My mother would smoke a cigarette too on such occasions. When she had put it out, they would talk about the furrier with his amputated legs, and the conversation always came round to the same subject: if my brother had been given more blood transfusions he might have survived. Had the doctors really done all they could to save his life? Or had they decided that he and his wounded legs rated only third-class treatment in a field hospital? For the wounded were treated according to their chances of survival. The more life-threatening the wounds, the later they got treatment. It saved the surgeons work. The severely wounded soon died of their injuries anyway. My brother had survived his operation, had lived another twenty-seven days, had written letters home from hospital.

Hadn't there been enough blood supplies available?

Had he, my parents wondered, been denied further treatment?

My father had written again to the staff doctor asking for detailed information. He was not happy with the brief notice of my brother's death – *we are sorry to say that we must inform you of the heroic death of your son.* He wanted to know more, wrote to the Death's Head Division, to the regiment. The answer that came said the company had been disbanded and its members assigned to other units. That meant it had been wound up and its men *verheizt*, burnt up, burnt out, sent to the slaughter. An SS battalion, an SS company burnt up. In Nazi parlance, they applied the term to their own men too.

My sister told me stories about our brother, about the games and pranks they played together. She told me how she, as the elder, had taken our brother to the cinema, how they had gone to the circus, and afterwards she had offered to turn him into a rabbit. But he had wanted to see her try it out on a neighbour's child first, to make quite sure she could turn him back again afterwards.

It is odd that he hardly mentions his sister in his letters. But he keeps asking after his little brother.

Letter to his father, 17 March 1943:

You write to say I mustn't tell Mutti when I write that I'm in the fighting. I can tell you that so far I haven't written home about it, and I won't in future either. Anyway, I'm not pot-hunting decorations, I've always told myself that's just stupid, I'm only carrying out orders and the rest of it is nothing to do with me — I mean, what use would it be to have the Iron Cross and only one hand? That would be the end of my life and my career.

My impression today, gleaned from memory, is that my father suffered more from the loss of his son than my mother. She had said goodbye to him in her grieving, her indignation found a focus, *that bunch of rogues*, she said, meaning the Nazis but also the military men, and by them she meant the top brass who made political decisions, who ruled us.

You look after a boy, you sit up with him every time he runs a temperature, oh, so much love, care and work went into bringing him up, and then he's just sent away and mutilated, and he dies.

My father could not allow himself to grieve, only to feel anger, but because he saw courage, duty, and tradition as inviolable virtues he directed his anger not at the real causes but only at military bunglers, shirkers, traitors. That was the subject of his conversation with his old comrades. They came round in the evening, sat together, drank coffee and cognac and talked about the war. They tried to find explanations for why it had been lost. Battles were fought all over again, wrong orders put right, incompetent generals dismissed, Hitler deprived of his command of the army. It is hardly imaginable now to think of that generation discussing such subjects all evening.

For a time my father wondered whether to join the Free Democratic Party or the nationalist German Party. He spoke well extempore, and was urged to join by acquaintances who were members of those parties themselves. He was interested in politics, but in the end could not make up his mind to be a member of any one party. He had never joined the NSDAP either, although his membership had been solicited. He had even been offered official positions – as I said, he was a good speaker. But the Nazis were *too loutish* for him.

At the beginning of the fifties, I think it was in 1952, he hired a chauffeur, a man who had driven him now and then during the war when he was with the Königsberg Luftwaffe detachment.

The boy called this chauffeur Massa. He had found the name in the colonial literature he bought at a secondhand bookshop with his pocket money. Books about the German and British colonies in Africa. Massa was what the blacks called their masters. My father found this amusing, and thereafter called the man by this nickname too. Before long the furriers and seamstresses he employed were doing the same. I don't know what Massa's real name was, even though he worked for my father for three years.

Massa wore a grey chauffeur's uniform and was a *factotum*. When it was time for coats to come out of store he delivered them to customers, he ran errands, drove my father to guild meetings, painted the doors of the shop and our apartment. And he was very loquacious, a man who could talk his way in anywhere. But he talked to children in the same way as he talked to adults, and took me seriously. Massa was a communist.

He was the first communist I ever met. A man with an enduring hatred for all those in authority, particularly the men he had worked for as a driver. He made an exception only for my father. I think there had been an occasion during the war when my father, as his superior officer, had protected Massa. I wish I knew when and how, and must be careful not to indulge in wishful thinking instead of describing what I actually remember.

Three years later my father had to get rid of Massa – *business is bad*. But he found him another job with an acquaintance, as a porter. My father had made good his claim: *I look after my people*.

At this time, when I was about fourteen, I became slowly but more and more acutely aware of the contradictions in my father's life. First there was the father who, if he bought shirts, ordered six of the same kind at once, or sent for a tailor who, as was the custom on the landed estates of the Eastern Elbe, spent two months working exclusively for our family, making clothes for my mother, trousers and jackets for me, and suits for my father, usually grey, light grey, mid-grey, dark grey. Uniform colours. He wore a handkerchief with blue or white spots in the breast pocket of his jacket, showing slightly but not too much. He kissed women's hands when he met them. He was a *good entertainer*, with a nice line in table talk. After the soup course he would tap his glass with his knife and propose a toast to the birthday boy or girl, the bridal couple, the guests of honour. At guild meetings or those of the body he had founded, the Syndicate of Hamburg Furriers, he spoke freely and in a way that made people listen. He could tell jokes. Never more than one at a time, and never a *smutty* joke. Usually they were about the great men of the Third Reich: Hitler, Goebbels, Göring, Ribbentrop. Reich Foreign Minister von Ribbentrop, considered particularly stupid and arrogant even by the Nazis themselves, had been invited to the jubilee cele- brations for the Queen of the Netherlands, along with other European foreign ministers. There was a great banquet. The Queen was suffering badly from flatulence that day, and broke wind audibly during the meal. The French foreign minister rose and said, I do apologise, your Majesty. The banquet continued. The Queen broke wind again. The British foreign minister rose and said: I do apologise, your Majesty. The banquet went on again. The Queen broke wind for the third time, very loudly. Reich Foreign Minister von Ribbentrop leaped up and shouted: Your Majesty! The Government of the German Reich will take responsibility for this one and the next three!

My father told this joke with a straight face, didn't stop to enjoy his audience's laughter but casually changed the subject and spoke of something else, something down- to-earth. The jokes were not an attempt to ingratiate himself. He drank to the other guests, holding his wine glass far down the stem. The conversation would become loud, the laughter of some of the women took on a shrill note. He would rise, sit down at the piano, and begin to play, improvising. The talking and laughter died down, people stood still, marvelling as they listened, cigarettes and wine glasses in their hands. Then he would briefly and rather theatrically raise his hands, with a slightly ironic gesture, close the piano lid, wave to the applauding company, stand up and take his cigarette case out of his jacket pocket, snap it open, take out a cigarette without looking, tap the cigarette briefly on it, snap the case shut and put it back in his jacket pocket. He struck a match with a quick movement; the lighting of the cigarette, the extinguishing of the match as he shook it out was all done with such ease, with small, elegant movements, always the same. He smoked holding the cigarette in fingers slightly spread apart, between his forefinger and middle finger. He wore his smoky topaz ring on his little finger.

His pride in his independence.

A popular figure, always welcome in company, interesting and amusing, that was my father.

But then there was the other father who sat over his business records in the evening, doing his accounts. Sighing, shaking his head, silently wringing his hands – he actually did rub and knead his hands slowly as if by doing so he could crush all his anxieties. My father's constantly perceptible fear, my mother's too, of losing their footing in middle-class life, of going down in the world. They feared the loss of their independence, though it had always been an independence borrowed from the banks.

And his telephoning. Morning calls to the banks to get credit extended. I have heard my father, who was so preoccupied with correct conduct, good behaviour, pride, his honour, obliged to beg for money on the phone, even from people he generally disliked, asking for 500 marks, 3000 marks, 5000 marks, a lot of money in 1954, sums he urgently needed to take to the bank so that his credit would remain good and be extended. *Extension*, a terrifying word. What would people think? He was constantly anxious about his status. Not in the superficial sense of what others thought of him, but as reflecting his own idea of himself, of what he was and what kind of figure he cut. The two always had to be balanced against each other. Nobility is something determined by birth, by *lineage*; a nobleman remains noble even if he goes broke, is condemned for some misdemeanour, loses his civil rights. But the ordinary citizen who fails in business and goes bankrupt is nothing any more, has lost his social standing. Hence that sense of punctiliousness, not to be confused with a sense of tact, which always takes account of other people. Punctilious observation of social form thinks only of itself; it is the fear of social failure. The punctilious are always seeing themselves from the outside, as they would imagine others see them. With a disapproving eye.

My father had to expose his most sensitive spot, his credit-worthiness, had to admit that his credit would be lost if he didn't get whatever sum it was he needed. And to have his credit fail anywhere would be a deadly blow, for then all the others to whom he owed money would call in their credit too, and none of it would be covered. Hence all the phoning, the requests, the begging from friends, colleagues, pleading with bank clerks, inferiors whose *skinny behinds*, he said, he would happily have kicked.

He could dress it up a little for himself with the word responsibility. Responsibility for *his people*, in the original sense of dependants, meaning not only members of his family but his labour force too. At the time that meant two furriers, six seamstresses and the chauffeur. And then there was the family: his wife, his unmarried daughter, his son the afterthought, and also his two sisters. Gone now was his grown-up son, my brother, who could have helped. He had been a furrier. My father's hopes now rested on me; I was some day to relieve him of his burden. I was to become a furrier too, I must be a furrier.

The extension of credit meant economic humiliation, and it always occurred in summer, in the *off season*. There were almost no new sales in summer. Hence the idea of *keeping furs in store*.

In spring the fur coats were fetched from my father's customers, beaten, and hung up in a room sprayed with an anti-moth substance. The spray could not be too strong, or later, when the coats were fetched in autumn, there was the risk of a penetrating smell of naphthalene. But if too little of the chemical was used moths might attack the coats. They were taken out of the store-room now and then in summer and beaten in the fresh air. Massa and the furrier's son fetched the coats from the customers and took them back in autumn. There were different grades of customer. A lady with only one coat had it fetched and delivered by Massa. Ladies who had several coats, or were important because they might recommend further customers, were visited by both the son and Massa. Massa, in his grey chauffeur's uniform, carried the coats, and the son, then thirteen years old, said: Good morning, kind regards from my father, here are your coats. Massa took his cap off and handed the coats over. The son was given a receipt for the return of the coats. His father distinguished between women who knew what was proper and women who didn't. Customers who knew what was proper gave Massa a tip. Those who didn't know gave the money to the boy.

Then I had to hand it over to Massa.

The income from storing furs by no means made up for the seasonal loss of earnings. Summer was the season when credit had to be extended. It was a time of phoning around and hand-wringing. Perhaps that was why he sent my mother and me off to the country in the school holidays, to the Lüneburger Heide or Petershagen on the Weser, where we spent five weeks in a hotel. He drove us in the Adler to Schneverdingen, the Hotel Witte, *the oldest house in the place.* A long brick building with window frames painted white. My father would stay for three days. We went hiking, or rather for gentle walks. We met British soldiers stationed in Soltau on an exercise. Out on the moorland paths my father was asked several times by soldiers about local places, roads, transport connections. He could have been taken for an Englishman in civilian clothes. A photo shows him in casual shoes, pale grey trousers, a pale shirt, a dark grey pullover. Observing manoeuvres in mufti.

Tanks stood at the edge of the forest camouflaged by nets. Very badly camouflaged, he said, pointing to the sand churned up by the tank tracks. They'd be visible from above. You only have to look closely at the place where the trail ends. It's best to bust tanks open from above. Ritter von Schleich destroyed the first in the First World War by dive-bombing. The Stuka principle, aiming the plane at them. Earlier my father had described at length, and with graphic gestures, how to tip the plane to the right or left over the wing. Now it was obvious that his thoughts were elsewhere. He smoked, he was a chain-smoker, he drank coffee and cognac in the afternoon. On the second day he went back to Hamburg.

Two weeks later my mother had to cut our holiday short. My father had fallen ill at home. Stomach pains, cramps, nausea, vomiting. A duodenal ulcer was diagnosed. This is one of my clearest memories because it was so unusual, so far from the image he had of himself; I see him lying in bed and changing his position constantly, following the doctor's advice. My mother is making gruel. Two years later he had a heart attack. After that, my mother said, he was different, a broken man. But I think that's how she interpreted a decline which had already set in. A heart attack as a physical reaction to his altered business circumstances. The utility economy of the post-war period was coming to an end. His skills were perfectly suited to the black market. In those days, when improvisation was necessary, you needed a *nose* for that kind of thing, you had to appear more than you really were, people were always gambling on the future, junk dealers became big industrialists, like Schlieker in Hamburg who later went bankrupt, and my father could be said to have been like Schlieker, but on a smaller scale.

For a brief period there was no need to have educational qualifications, certificates, reports, diplomas, none of which he could produce. The qualities in demand were skill, ideas, good connections, vision, the art of persuasion. It smacked of the American way of life, which he hated, but it suited his incomplete education, his whole existence.

You find an old fur-sewing machine, you clean and oil it and open a furrier's shop. He had acquired the squirrel skins from a Russian officer in a complicated barter operation, he made them up into a coat by following the instructions in a manual called *The German Furrier*, and then he sold it, or rather bartered it, to the wife of an English major. The major was supervising the clearance of the Lauenburger Forest. The timber was going to Great Britain as war reparations. My father got several metres of planking *diverted for his use* in return for that squirrel coat, and immediately bartered them again in exchange for cigarettes, butter, sugar, clothes and more skins.

This period, when small and very small businesses could get by through improvisation, inventiveness, and making happy discoveries, came to an end in the mid-fifties. People now wanted better quality, even in furs: choice, expensive fur coats were in demand, beaver, ocelot, lynx. Skins that were beyond his financial means. The cut of the coats and the way they were finished changed too. He was not a trained furrier, and by now was no longer working on the coats himself. But even the two furriers he employed could not design an elegant cut for fur stoles, capes and coats.

He was a good salesman. He acted as if selling wasn't his job, as if he were just doing a favour. Tall, slim, blond, tanned in summer, bright blue eyes, a *charming conversationalist* with good social manners, that was his capital. When I look at the photographs from his youth I suspect that he acquired it during his time in the Baltic with the Freikorps, from mingling with his aristocratic companions.

At home neither his resolute but unsophisticated mother nor the uncle and aunt with whom he grew up in Coburg could have provided him with that kind of social model. As long as he was a good-looking, interesting, entertaining conversationalist many women customers came on his account, and insisted on being served exclusively by him. These were customers who didn't have to worry about the price of a fur, and as styles gradually became more fashionable they moved away and went to the big, elegant stores in the city centre, to Levermann, the largest of the Hamburg furriers, where I was to train, and Berger, whose extravagant designs were regarded as particularly chic. If it had a Berger label, a fur coat could be sold off the peg at Jacobs even inside out, with only its lining and label showing. The Timm Furs label – I still have a roll of them – was less impressive in spite of the flourish of the initial letters. The coats, jackets and stoles with our label were of sound workmanship but plain: their cut was not refined, there were no spectacular silver-blue or topaz mink coats with skins worked together diagonally, no natural broadtail.

Business was going badly, turnover was down, and my father, who had now dismissed the chauffeur, drove into the city centre and looked at the windows of the stores where the first mink coats were now on display, considerably cheaper than he himself could ever have made them. These coats, which called for long hours at the sewing machine, were made in Yugoslavia and Greece, countries where wages were low.

What a botched job, he said, take a look at that, the fur sewn in, you can see it quite clearly, and the stripes all crooked and out of shape. He stood in front of the shop window muttering: someone ought to complain, this is unfair competition. They're ruining the trade. And at that moment he became the old crock he had scornfully called others, but had hoped he himself would never be.

If only Karl-Heinz were here.

My brother had wanted lace-up boots of the kind then worn by pilots, motorbike riders, SA men. He saved up his pocket money until he could buy the boots. One picture shows him in his Hitler Youth uniform with the boots coming right up above his calves. They were laced through hooks on both sides. He wanted to go to Africa. But you couldn't choose to go and join Rommel.

When I was fourteen, after a tough battle lasting several months and with the support of my mother and Massa,

I was allowed to buy my first pair of jeans. I went into town in those jeans, walking differently, more slowly, with the kind of casual gait that my father did not like; he praised the marching step of the German infantry. I went to the Amerikahaus, which then stood beside the Inner Alster lake. They showed films and lent books there. I learned about the USA from illustrated volumes. Photographs of the forests, high-rise buildings, lakes, farms, the coasts: a country promising wide open spaces, conveying a sense of distance. The opposite of our world of rubble, cramped and restrictive, with its rules and prescriptions. I read Hemingway, bought a corduroy shirt to go with the jeans. And a blank notebook bound in red vinyl bearing the word Diary. If I leaf through it I see writing in ink, handwriting which I vaguely recognise as mine, its small and curiously angular characters trying to put my daydreams into words: herds of buffalo, waterfalls, giant trees. That word: skyscraper.

My adolescent wish was to live in America for a while, if not actually to emigrate. In the Amerikahaus it presented itself as a country where the sun almost always shone, a land flowing with milk and honey. Everything seemed practical, simple, well made. Like the two shirts my father found in the Care parcel. The woman who washed and ironed them praised their quality. The cuffs had buttons: they didn't need to be folded back and held together with cuff-links. Putting in the links was a fiddly job that my mother or I did for my father.

My mother kept that particularly stout cardboard carton bearing the letters C.A.R.E. She used it to store the

Christmas tree baubles saved from the bombing in 1943. Only gradually, over the years, did some of them get broken as they were packed up and unpacked again, until the very last of them and the carton itself perished in a fire at our home in 1999.

My parents' set phrase for what had happened to them was *a blow dealt by fate*, a fate beyond the reach of personal influence. *Our boy and our home both lost*: it was the kind of remark that saved you having to think about the reasons. You felt that with that suffering you had done your bit for the general atonement. Everything was *dreadful* for the very reason that you had been a *victim* yourself, the victim of a collective and inexplicable fate. There were demonic forces at work outside history, or else they were part of human nature, but at any rate they were catastrophic and inescapable. Decisions to which you could only submit. And you felt that fate had treated you unfairly.

How did my brother see himself? What were his feelings? Did he acknowledge anything like personal responsibility, guilt, injustice?

In his drawings and letters there is only one indication that he may have questioned the myth of the upright, brave Waffen SS man, a myth later disseminated by the old soldiers' associations, but also cultivated at home by our parents.

On 25 July 1943 he writes in a letter from the Ukraine, from near Konstantinovka:

We have moved into excellent quarters, it's clean and neat just like at home. And there are lots of pretty young girls here – but you don't need to worry, I'll try to pick one of them up – no, I mean, I won't try to pick one of them up . . .

It seems the people in these parts haven't had anything to do with the SS before. They were all glad to see us, waved, brought us fruit etc., so far there's only been Wehrmacht quartered here.

There are two pressed pinks with this letter; the petals have left a trace of colour on the paper, a pale shade of rose. The flowers have been lying with this letter for sixty years; they come from an area where people were glad to see the Germans because they hadn't met any of the SS before. Perhaps a Ukrainian girl gave him the pink. And there's that comment, meant to be funny, but playfully betraying his wishful thinking: *I won't try to pick one of them up . . .*

It was strictly forbidden for SS men to have relationships with Ukrainian women and girls. The master race was not to mingle with the inferior Slavs.

There is a place in the diary where he writes: *We're demolishing the stoves in Russian houses to build roads.*

Evidently the stone surrounds of stoves in the wooden houses were being taken out and used to pave the roads for trucks. This is a theme which runs all through the diary: *We set out, but after 500 m we have to turn back, vehicles can't get through the mud. They have to be pushed every 100 m. Road worse can hardly get along.*

Demolishing the stoves meant wrecking the houses. What did the people say? Did they weep? Did they try, in desperation, to make the Germans understand the horrors of having no stove in the coming winter?

He writes it down without for a moment seeing any parallel between the destruction of houses in the Ukraine and the bombed buildings in Hamburg . . . *I'm worried about everyone at home, we hear reports of air raids by the English every day. If only they'd stop that filthy business. It's not war, it's the murder of women and children – it's inhumane.*

It is hard to comprehend and impossible to trace the way in which sympathy and compassion in the face of suffering could be blanked out, while a distinction emerged between humanity at home and humanity here in Russia. In Russia, the killing of civilians is normal, everyday work, not even worth mentioning, at home it is murder.

When he wrote this he was nineteen years and three months old and had two more months to live. He had completed an apprenticeship. He had been in the Jungvolk and the Hitler Youth. Scouting games. Shooting practice. Night marches. He'd had *the corners knocked off him*, as the phrase went. At eighteen he did his labour service: in the autumn of 1942 he was building roads outside Stalingrad, then he went to France to train with the Waffen SS and had yet more corners knocked off him. Then, in January 1943, he was posted to Russia.

He would have liked to learn to dance, he wanted to take a course, said our sister. But there was no time for that. And he'd have liked to learn gliding. To fly was his greatest wish.

Once in his diary he mentions a special meal.

29 July
slept in the village, we must be at the ready tomorrow. 6–8 preparing artillery.
8 o'clock, attack gets fiercer
ferocious mortar fire. Rösch and Herzfeld wnded. We bring the wnded infantry back in recce cars
this afternoon we go to clear mines – mines have to be cleared in front of the tanks. Terrific firing from Ivan. Our tanks fire over our heads. Uscha [Unterscharführer] Wagner badly wnded. 6 men clear 59 mines – going back with wnded.
Mortar attack near recce cars. Schwarz and I wnded – go to wnd-dressing station. 5 cm³ injection, bandaged up, both of us sent back to supply column – slept overnight in military hostel – had rolls and jam at wnd-dressing station.

I have now read other diaries and letters of the time; some observe the suffering of the civilian population and express outrage, others speak of the killing of civilians – Jews and Russians alike – as the most natural thing in the world. The language they've been taught makes killing easier: inferior human beings, parasites, vermin whose lives are dirty, degenerate, brutish. Smoking them out is a hygienic measure.

I find no express justification of killing in my brother's

diary, nothing resembling the ideological instruction given to the SS. It is just a *normal* view of daily life in war.

He gives carefully adjusted and different accounts of the fighting when he writes to our mother, to our father, and when he records events in his diary. Both father and son had agreed not to let our mother know he was already fighting at the front; the idea was to *spare* her.

Letter to our mother of 22 July 1943:

It'll be sad in a way if we never go into action, we'll never be eligible for medals, we'll always be seen as greenhorns.

But you know that I don't mind too much about that, the main thing is to get home safe and sound.

By this time he had been in action for months, had taken part in the recapture of Kharkov and in July he had fought in the battle of Kursk, an event which was quickly scribbled into his diary fourteen days before he wrote to our mother. You can tell from the handwriting which parts were entered as he drove along in a tank or truck, and which in a trench or in his quarters. It was all written with a pencil that still lies in that little box. Sometimes the syntax dissolves, becomes garbled, mutilated, there is hardly any punctuation, the writing is blurred.

5 July
0.30 Move to assembly area. 3–4 hrs getting artillery and flame-throwers ready. From 4 Stukas attack Death's Head units over minefield solo motorbikes can't get across blown-up tank

trenches over Russian trenches 2 sets of bunkers etc. tanks moving through stream. Tigers stuck nothing to eat, charging explosives away from bridge, bridge mended wood-cased mines blown up hand grenade Tiger tracks wrecked. Night on taxi-way position. Kursk – Byegorod

6 July
Drive to new attack area. Can't get through. Around 4 o'clock 73 Russian & English tanks attack heavy great things Michel's vehicle takes hit from tank blows right up in air bits of engine parts and armour plating for 400 metres our vehicle burning, all get out Berg Janke and I stay in I throw out all the burning stuff step on the gas out of the sea of flames try to get tank out of the Russian firing line we're out. Wilhelm (dead) Gerd Klöpfer wnded.

7 July
still moving to assembly area our tanks can't get through here go left to attack.

8 July
We go back to company. Horrible. Straight off again to tank R. way lost spend night on taxi-way

9 July
Arrive at tank Dicomp. After two hours march to new post, spend night in wood, aircraft coming over what a racket.

10 July
No action. Stay in wood. Eat well.

11 July
Wait during day. I'm on guard. Leaving. Arrive in assembly area tomorrow.

12 July
Sitting it out. Felling trees so tanks get through
Take up position in evening

13 July
Artillery fire in consolidated position. 2 m from gap 17.2 at noon 3T-34s pass gap we must retreat enormously superior forces Kriel and Jauch wounded, missing
Fierce artillery and MG firing on us by Russians Schwarz, Konig, Reinecke and I get through around 2 a.m. Lemke and I go out to fetch Kriel and Jauch. Shot hits steel helmet. MG no good we must retreat
Slept well.

He had been in the middle of the battle of Kursk, where the three so-called elite divisions were in action, the SS Das Reich, Leibstandarte and Death's Head divisions. My father said, and so did military historians, that Kursk rather than Stalingrad had been the turning point of the war.

My father read historical works and the memoirs of generals and Luftwaffe officers that were published at the beginning of the fifties. General Galland: *Die Ersten und die Letzten – Jagdflieger im Zweiten Weltkrieg* [The First and the Last – Fighter Pilots in the Second World War]. Guderian, General of Armoured Troops: *Erinnerungen eines*

Soldaten [Memoirs of a Soldier]. And above all, *Verlorene Siege* [Lost Victories] by Field Marshal von Manstein, who seeks to show in his 664-page book that the Wehrmacht in general and he in particular would have operated extremely successfully had not Hitler, *der Gefreite* [the lance-corporal], interfered by giving his own orders. Von Manstein dwells at length on the battle of Kursk.

The German offensive began on 5 July 1943 with 900,000 German soldiers, 10,000 artillery pieces, 1,026 tanks and 1,830 aircraft. These forces faced 1.3 million Red Army soldiers with 20,300 artillery pieces, 3,600 tanks and 2,600 aircraft. On 10 July, we are told, two avalanches of tanks were rolling towards each other south of Kursk. Towards evening, hundreds of burning vehicles of both armies covered the battlefield. But it was not yet certain who would regain the initiative. On 13 July my brother writes in his diary: *No good. We must retreat.* That same day there was a meeting between Hitler and Field Marshal von Kluge, commanding Army Group Central, and Field Marshal von Manstein, commander of Army Group South. Von Kluge wanted to break off the battle, von Manstein wanted to carry on. Von Manstein based his wish to continue the operation on the heavy losses suffered by the Red Army. Casualties were estimated at around 70,000, including 17,000 dead. There were 34,000 prisoners, and 6,547 had deserted. The attacking German formations had lost 3,300 men, with 7,420 wounded – losses that were later to rise to 20,720.

Hitler chose to compromise by allowing von Kluge to retreat and von Manstein to continue with the attack. In his book, von Manstein holds Hitler ultimately responsible for losing the war.

It is scarcely imaginable today that, after the war, and in full knowledge of the systematic murder – *the elimination* – of the Jews, there could have been any serious public discussion about how the war might after all have been won.

There were discussions like this at home too when former wartime comrades met, armchair strategists who always brought the conversation back to the crucial turning points and watersheds of the war: the flawed decisions made by Hitler, Göring, Field Marshal Keitel (nicknamed Lakeitel, 'lackey Keitel', for the way he crawled to Hitler). A change of strategy. Suddenly, the Luftwaffe was ordered to attack civilian targets – London, Coventry, Bristol and Swansea – instead of continuing to bomb airfields and aircraft factories, thus gaining air supremacy for the forthcoming invasion. And they kept reverting to Dunkirk, around which rumours proliferated, linked as so often to anti-Semitic conspiracy theories. Why did Hitler halt the XIIth Tank Corps outside Dunkirk? He thereby enabled the British Expeditionary Force to get away to England with 200,000 men. And then there was the crucial error of delaying the attack on the Soviet Union until 21 June 1941 because of the preceding invasion and occupation of Yugoslavia. Five crucial weeks were lost. The troops were outside Moscow when winter began, and so on. Phrases such as *Order of Frozen Flesh*, the *Hitler Saw* (a type of machine gun), *a blighty wound* (a wound not endangering life, but serious enough to get the victim sent home on leave) accompanied my childhood, illus-trating the impoverishment of language and linguistic repression alike.

The magazines and old soldiers' journals, cheap pamphlets with accounts of real-life experiences, also concentrated on the war. These accounts echoed the camaraderie of the troops in the SS Death's Head Division: *The Russian tanks must have dynamite on board, that's the only explanation for those huge explosions. Tank tracks weighing a hundredweight are flung great distances through the air. We manage to hold back the attack which came at us out of the blue. The sappers ahead of us suffer heavy losses. They attacked the tanks and busted them open with limpet bombs. But no cover is enough when the tanks explode. Some of the sappers were killed by pieces of iron flying through the air.*

The adventure of war. The Wehrmacht as travel agent, a foreshadowing of future tourism by the wealthy. Even the humble private returned a victor, a master. The way in which he talked about the places where he had been, even after defeat, was still influenced by the desire to enrich himself, a desire which had not least provided the emotional force behind wars of conquest. Salmon from Norway, good butter from Denmark, and then – of course – there was France: silk stockings, truffles, wine, cham-pagne. *As soldiers the Frenchies weren't up to much, but their lifestyle – wow!* And their women? *Terrific!*

How about the East? The East was a big place. Grain, mineral resources, all on a large scale. Fleas, impassable roads, obliging people. No discipline. Just look inside a

Russian cottage. You wouldn't believe it. The East meant *Lebensraum*, room for expansion. Places for SS veterans to live, the future owners of farms. Pretty half-timbered farmhouses were already being planned by the settlement commissioners. You could go and look at the models. But there were still millions of Russians, Poles, Ukrainians and Jews living in the land that was to be settled. There were solutions for that too: resettlement for the inferior Slavs, and *the final solution of the Jewish problem*. Final solution. A term that will be held in contempt for ever, and proof of the fact that even the German language has lost its innocence, innocence in the literal sense of freedom from guilt. In the same way, there were all those abbreviations, some of them branded on the language and unforgotten – the SS, the SD, the SA – others now only to be found in specialist encyclopaedias: the RFSS (*Reichsführer-SS*, i.e. Himmler) OBH (*Oberbefehlshaber des Heeres*, supreme commander of the army), RuSHA (*Rasse- und Siedlung-shauptamt*, Main Race and Resettlement Office) – a subversion of the language that cast a shadow well into the post-war period. Army terminology, linguistic mutilations that found their counterpart in physical injury: men limping, on crutches, an empty jacket sleeve fastened with a safety pin, trouser legs turned up, squeaking artificial limbs.

My father was in the Luftwaffe. He used to talk about it, about his reconnaissance flights over Finland and Russia. The Luftwaffe, he said, had nothing to do with the murder of the Jews. It had only fought bravely. And yet – and this became the subject of early and dogged arguments

– yet the Luftwaffe too, every one of those brave, decent fighting men, had helped to keep mass murder going on an industrial scale. We knew nothing about it. The upright Luftwaffe. The upright Navy. The upright Wehrmacht. The upright Waffen SS.

The fear that accompanied me in my researches was of finding that my brother's tank unit, the SS 3rd Engineers Armoured Battalion, and thus my brother too, had taken part in the shooting of civilians, Jews, hostages.

But as far as I could discover, that was not the case. It was just normal everyday wartime life: *75 m away Ivan smoking cigarettes, fodder for my MG.*

The Waffen SS wore the same uniform as the SS guards in the concentration camps.

My father's generation, the generation of the guilty, lived by either talking about it or saying nothing at all. There seemed to be only those two options: either you kept discussing it or you never mentioned it, depending on how oppressive and disturbing you felt your memories to be.

The women and old people talked about the nights of air raids at home. The terror was broken down into details, made comprehensible, domesticated. It was dissipated, usually by anecdotes told in cosy company. Only very seldom, and then very suddenly, did the horror come through.

I once saw my father standing by the stove, his hands behind his back, held out to the warmth. He was crying. I had never seen him shed tears before. *Boys don't cry.* He was not just weeping for his dead son, something unspeakable was dissolving in his tears. As he stood there crying, some terrible memory was surfacing from the depths of despair, not self-pity but unutterable grief, and when I asked questions he just kept shaking his head.

What images were preying on his mind? Perhaps something he saw in a camp for Russian POWs was just one example of the horror, one that could be put into words and told, and he did tell it. A Russian prisoner had tried to escape and the guard fired at him, blasting the top off the man's skull, whereupon other prisoners fell on the dead man and ate his steaming brain. For a terrible moment I suspected that my father had fired the shot himself, but then I told myself that was very unlikely, for a man of his rank. He didn't even go on duty with a rifle.

When I began working on this attempt to write about my brother, I read Christopher R. Browning's book *Ordinary Men: Reserve Police Battalion 101 and the Final Solution in Poland*. What Browning shows, on the evidence of statements from trials of men still living at the time, is that when the order came to shoot Jewish civilians, men, women and children, they could have refused to obey it without fearing disciplinary punishment. There were instances of men who did refuse, even in that battalion. However, only twelve, out of some five hundred soldiers, stepped forward, handed in their rifles and were put on other duties.

Those who did not refuse – and it must be said that this was almost all of them – those who did not say no, who obeyed, killed, after initial reservations, more naturally, more ruthlessly, more mechanically every time. One has to force oneself to read these descriptions. They did the inconceivable.

Between July 1942 and November 1943, according to Official Reports, 38,000 Jews were shot by the men of Reserve Police Battalion 101.

In 1967 the trial of fourteen members of the battalion opened in Hamburg. Three officers were sentenced to eight years in prison each, two NCOs also received prison sentences, one of five and one of six years. The other defendants walked free from court. None of them showed any awareness of having done wrong. In their defence they all cited obedience to orders. Their sentences were greatly reduced later.

In an army order dated 20 November 1941 and sent on to all regiments and battalions, General von Manstein, later to be Field Marshal and commander of Army Group South, in which my brother fought, wrote: *The Jewish-Bolshevik system must be eradicated once and for all. Never again must it interfere with our European Lebensraum.*

Field Marshal von Manstein, that notable strategist, advised the post-war Federal German government on the construction of its army. He claimed that Hitler's mistakes in leadership had lost Germany the war, and wrote at length in his book *Verlorene Siege* on his own plans, concepts, decisions and orders, but he does not mention that one: *The Jewish-Bolshevik system must be eradicated once and for all.*

There is nothing about prisoners in my brother's diary or his letters. Why were they not worth mentioning?

I've found a fine Random pistol, I'll take it home with me, I always wanted one like that; it's a pistol with a triple safety catch and you can release the trigger with the ball of your hand, so it's excellent, a fine brown holster with it too. Now I have two pistols, a 1.08 and a Polish army Random.

I have plenty of ammunition for it too, because it uses the same as the 08.

You wait and see how well I can shoot with it, better than with a rifle. I'll shoot you down those little china things at the top of telegraph poles one by one.

Well, that's all for now, dear Mutti, write again soon.

In *The Drowned and the Saved*, Primo Levi tells us how dreadful it was to get no letters in the camps, no news of friends and relations – which would have been impossible anyway in the case of the Jewish prisoners, for relations and friends were either in another camp themselves or had already been killed. It was this silence, this sense of abandonment, that added even more to all the humiliations, the hunger, the disease, thirst and the loss of solidarity among the prisoners. A deep sense of abandonment arising from the knowledge that no one remembered you any more.

Well, that's all for now, dear Mutti, write again soon.

Almost everyone looked away and said nothing when their Jewish neighbours were taken off, simply disappeared, and most maintained that silence after the war when they learned where they had disappeared to.

Primo Levi sees the deepest guilt of the Germans in this silence. They were *deathly silent*, and that was more terrible than the wordy speeches of those who tried to exculpate themselves by protesting that they knew nothing. The latter repelled young people – as I remember very well – when they started to enumerate the reasons why they couldn't have known, as if under a compulsion to justify themselves, often unasked. At least a voice of conscience spoke within them, telling them that they ought to have found ways of knowing.

Theirs was not just an injured but a sick generation, one that had repressed its traumas and channelled them into an ostentatious reconstruction. What had happened was translated into stereotypes: Hitler the criminal. Language was publicly misused not just by the killers but by those who said of themselves, *well, we got off again*. They slipped into the victim's role under false pretences.

I first saw my father drunk on an excursion to the Lüneburger Heide. The furriers' guild went to Sudermühlen early in spring when the first asparagus was being cut. They had lunch, plenty of asparagus, potatoes and ham with white wine, some kind of Mosel or Rhine wine, Katzenstriegel or Liebfraumilch or something of the sort. We ate in the garden of the inn; it was a day of warm sun with a light east wind still giving the air a touch of winter chill. My mother had brought her mink stole. My father, who was chairman of some guild committee or other, sat at a long table with a white table-cloth, and talked to his colleagues and their wives. There was a great deal of laughter, and he laughed too, very loud. The child I was then liked the atmosphere. The grown-ups seemed to have forgotten their power. My father, as he said later in the car, had been particularly merry. Massa had driven us, because the guests included fur dealers with whom he had to extend his credit, so nothing must show that money couldn't be spent freely. *Money was in plentiful supply*.

But this state of merriment recurred more and more often, although my father wasn't really merry: he was quieter when he had been drinking, less talkative and ultimately more apathetic. Even in the afternoon he would go to one of the inns also frequented by his friends and acquaintances; they met for a beer or a glass of wine, they said, but then it turned into several beers or glasses of wine, and later, around 1957 or 1958, they began drinking spirits, in my father's case cognac. Undoubtedly his nagging anxieties were among his reasons for drinking. The decline of his business, his growing debts, it was all too much for him. Herr Kotte lacked the knowledge and ability to make up the new styles of furs now in demand, and so did my father. Karl-Heinz was badly missed. He was missed not just as the professional craftsman his father was not, but as his mainstay, the boy who was not only his son but his friend and comrade, someone who realised all his own wishes and yet was considerate and loving to others – that was how the elder son lived on for ever in his father's memory.

That word *ability*. I, the afterthought, did not yet have the professional ability to run the workshop, design patterns, instruct apprentices – I was in the second year of my own training in 1956. But I had enough ability to recognise my father's lack of it, his failure. My brother would surely have seen it too, but probably from a different perspective, one that took into account the whole period of the war, the bombing of the family home, imprisonment, the new beginning.

My brother's very absence preserved his admiration of our father, and thus also preserved the image our father once had of himself. It was not just he who had failed, but the collective *system of values* too. And he himself, like all the others – like almost everyone except those few who put up resistance – had helped to destroy those values. The reaction was either defiance or suppression. My father defused persistent questioning by saying: you have no idea. You don't know what it was like. But my brother did know. He had suffered it all. He had sacrificed himself.

My father's insistence that experience was an absolute value – *you have to have been through it* – worked against him professionally. From year to year I became more competent in everything to do with the trade, so that if he started explaining the problems of making a mink coat to me I could only laugh. And I did. And of course he was aware of his own incompetence, which only made him react more imperiously. He often mingled the political and the professional in a complicated way, each using the other as its point of departure. He was opinionated. We quarrelled more and more fiercely, and ended up shouting at each other. I came home late in the afternoon from the firm where I was training – which had become the biggest furrier in Hamburg by buying up Aryanised businesses on the cheap – home being my father's shop, and would find my father looking out, waiting, for customers. If a woman passed the display window he slowly took a step or two back so as not to be seen.

At the end of the fifties he escaped from this waiting more and more frequently to go for a coffee and several cognacs in one of the nearby bars. In the end it was generally the Bei Papa Geese, a small inn two blocks away. Only four or five years earlier its downmarket name alone would have kept him from going there. He was in flight not just from his wait for custom, which grew increasingly long, but from another kind of waiting too: he was waiting for something that became ever smaller, ever fainter, ever further away – an entirely different life, adventurous and risky, a life of many surprises, a full and happy life. So he went to Papa Geese, which was quite close; if an important customer did come he could be fetched. Then he would suck one of the peppermints, Dr Hiller's Mints, that he kept in the pocket of his white coat, which he always wore unbuttoned.

How did my mother bear it, when she had known him as a sociable man, an engaging charmer? Self-controlled and always friendly as she was, how did she cope with it? She tried to protect him, my powerful father, without giving the slightest sign that she hated to see him drunk, walking unsteadily, dropping heavily into a chair and sitting there, with ash scattered all over the desk, his burning cigarette sometimes falling from his hand. Come along, Hans, time for bed. Not the slightest sign to me or my sister, no turning of the eyes to heaven, no comment, not even when he actually had gone to bed, no head-shaking, no comment at all.

He hurt inside, and it was difficult to name the cause of his pain, the burden of accumulated disappointments, the way he had become indifferent to everything, the slow attrition of his wishes. He no longer read. He told stories only occasionally, and then only when he had been drinking. He rose late in the morning. His tie, which he had always scrupulously knotted and straightened, now hung below his top button, which he left undone. In the shop he would sit in a chair and look out at the summer through the open door. But as he sat there, looking out, he was no longer waiting for customers.

My mother was running the business at this time, and taking over more and more of the jobs in the workshop. She had nothing to do with *all that financial stuff*, my father still dealt with that. But she knew that their independence was threatened.

To make your way through life with decorum.

Elim. Twelve springs of water and eighty-six palm trees in the desert. An oasis of rest.

This morning, 6 March, I did my warming-up exercises and then started running when the sun had just risen. A cloudless sky, still a dim grey-blue. The trees and bushes, their light green still translucent, the first white blossoms of wild cherry among them.

I ran along the Eisbach, which flows towards a small waterfall. The song of the thrushes echoing above everything, the metallic chatter of the chaffinches. It was chilly, only just above freezing. I ran through the English Garden, over to the lawn where a single tall lime tree stands. Its shadow on the lawn was white. Hoar frost. Its lower twigs and branches were already covered with the first shimmer of green. A little terracotta figure of the Virgin was wedged into a bulging knothole in the mighty trunk. A shining patch of blue in the brown bark.

Even as I ran I knew that today I would be able to do something I had been putting off for weeks; I would write about her.

My mother survived my father by thirty-three years. She lived to the age of eighty-nine. Every time we spoke on the telephone her voice surprised me, it sounded so young, her clear laughter was so unchanged. That voice, and above all that laughter, could have been a young girl's. She would tell me about little things that had happened, people she had met, although not so much happened to her now as before, when she still had the shop.

She told stories with a good sense of humour. I liked her laughter, so physically close, even now the thought of her laughter brings her before my eyes, she is sitting in one of the Chippendale chairs acquired at the time when *business was good* and laughing, leaning slightly back in her typical posture, raising her right hand, tapping it gently on her thigh. There was never any malice in her laughter. Her eye for oddities, for something unusual, was not spiteful but only registered what was out of the ordinary, the great potential of life. She gave such oddities names, as she gave our customers names, and if you met the women she had nicknamed you immediately saw what she meant: Whooping Emma, Swimming in Cash, Sporty Legs. She linked observations, experiences and anecdotes with the names, enriching them with new observations and creating her own subversive parallel universe. As she grew older her voice took on more and more of a Hamburg accent. But perhaps it was that, living in Munich, I had become unused to the Hamburg dialect, and so I noticed the way she lingered on her vowel sounds very clearly.

One afternoon my sister phoned, in tears, hardly able to speak clearly. Our mother had suffered a stroke and had been taken to the Elim hospital.

She was sharing a room with a retired schoolmistress. The nurse, a woman in late middle age with an East Prussian accent, said: Talk to her, talking is important. I sat by her bedside and told her about my flight, talked about the children. Slowly and as if from a great distance she regained consciousness, looked at me, held out her right hand, such a light, slender hand, yet it pressed mine firmly. The left side of her face had slipped, and there was a tic running down the right side.

She lay there paralysed down one side, her mouth making babbling sounds, but she pressed my hand three times, briefly, with the fingers of her own right hand. It was the signal between us when as a child I used to walk through town with her and there was something we wanted to point out to each other without speaking: a woman wearing a funny feathered hat, a man with a nervous tic.

We used to walk through the city centre, and once a week we went to a café in the Gänsemarkt or to the Alsterpavillon. We sat and ate cream cakes, she drank coffee, I had cocoa, and even today I prefer to sit in cafés where elderly ladies in cloche hats meet. We sat among the cake-eating, chattering customers, wondering what these women did, where they came from, whether they had children, whether their husbands were still alive, what their professions had been. It was touching to note the pleasure she took in inventing things, guessing at people's histories. Then we went home. She always wore a hat and gloves when she went out, white cotton gloves in summer, and she would remove one of them, the right-hand glove, to take my hand.

A photograph shows her parents in the sitting room of their house, still furnished in the style of the 1870s, with a piano, a large display cabinet, pictures, patterned wallpaper, comfortably prosperous and with some fashionable later additions: the Art Nouveau desk and lamps. My grandfather must have been making a lot of money then: that was the time when everyone wore hats, large, broad-brimmed hats with peacock feathers, and later, after the war, cloche hats came into fashion. Unless they came from the country, women wore hats, as my mother did into extreme old age.

My grandfather is sitting in an armchair, cigar in hand, and beside him is the woman he married after his first wife died – my mother was two years old at the time – a small, shapeless woman with what can only be described as a piercingly unpleasant look in her eyes. No one could understand why he had chosen this wife, who could do only one thing: she was a good housekeeper. Perhaps that was exactly his reason for marrying her, to help him save his money and make more. She was my mother's step-mother, and thus my step-grandmother. As a child I avoided her, and in spite of admonitions I wouldn't let her kiss me or sit me on her lap. A woman full of malice, avarice, fond of slander and spite, to my mother a true wicked stepmother straight from a fairy tale. She would shut the child in the broom cupboard for minor misdemeanours, and told tales about her to her father, who was seldom at home. She punished the little girl by depriving her of meals, so that the maids sometimes slipped her something on the sly. Fried potatoes were among the child's favourite foods, and once, when she was alone in the house, she made them for herself. Her stepmother came back and caught the little girl in the kitchen washing out the pan. Because she had made herself those fried potatoes without permission she wasn't allowed to eat any for a year, and when the others ate them she had to sit and watch.

How is it that, against all the odds, that child became such a kindly, good-natured woman, hating lies, delicate in build yet very strong and tenacious, with a strength that offered unconditional protection to those she loved?

I stayed in Hamburg for several days, visited her, came at mealtimes, carefully put the spoon of gruel in her mouth when she nodded gently. She couldn't chew, she could only swallow slowly. As I came and went she gave me that signal with her fingers, a loving pressure spelling out our understanding.

Then, one morning, she wasn't in the same room any more. The woman there said she had been moved. Why? She said she didn't know, but I could tell that she was embarrassed.

My mother had been *transferred*. When she came into the hospital they had thought, or hoped, that she had private health insurance, so she had been placed in the medical director's private ward. But in fact the company she was insured with provided only limited cover, so she had been *downgraded*, put in a six-bed ward. That down-grading after a life of so much hard work struck me as typical of the system.

Hospitals, the pecking order of health insurance companies. I asked the price of the private room and private treatment. It was high. I thought it over. In addition, I was told, all further examinations would have to be paid for privately too. These were sums of money I simply did not have. So she stayed in the six-bed ward. She saw my sadness, my indignation, indeed my shame at being unable to do anything about her change of status. She pressed my hand, tried to smile, a weary, lopsided smile.

The odd thing about her downgrading was that she had been moved from the ground floor to the first floor, where she had brought me into the world fifty-one years before. And here she was in a sunny room with friendly nurses, and lacked for nothing. She heard the other patients laughing and talking, heard all the strange case histories that were people's life histories too.

I sat beside her bed, giving her a drink now and then from a cup with a spout. A large Spanish family had gathered around the bed next to hers. There was much laughter and talking. The visitors ate ham and olives, tore chunks off a loaf of white bread, wrapped them in slices of ham, offered me some.

The peace and deep calm I felt emanating from my mother was so surprising that now and then I pressed her hand just to get a little reaction. Most of the time I said nothing, but sometimes I talked to her about life at home, the children, Dagmar, my work. She lay looking at the window. She held her head to one side, as the stroke had left it, but she could still look out of the window. Perhaps the nurses had chosen this bed on purpose so that she didn't have to stare at the wall. Now and then her right hand, which still had sensation, groped for the left hand which felt nothing, yet it was still warm and full of life. Then, suddenly, she yawned, a yawn such as I had never seen her give; she usually put her hand in front of her mouth with a little patting movement. Now I saw that mouth wide open, and in it, like an alien object, her tongue, a deep blue.

Sun. Window. Hand. Hands. Two hands. Fingers. Eyelid. The strain of uttering sounds, of saying tomorrow, the enormous effort of saying the day after tomorrow.

She slowly recovered, could articulate a few words. What remained to her, even in her infirmity, was an understanding but remote attitude to her surroundings – her sense of humour. On a visit to the hospital one afternoon I found the other women in the ward, all of them elderly, in a state of great agitation. An old man had come into the room the night before who was said to wander around the women's ward. My mother, who obviously understood everything they were saying, just shook her head, tapped her forehead with her sound hand and made the gesture she always did when someone was talking too much, thumb and forefinger moving up and down like a bird's beak. And then, with difficulty and only after I had twice asked her to repeat it, she said audibly: *They wish!*

The nurse came in, said only: Oh, him, old Ehlers – old Ehlers a peeping Tom? No, he just has a few screws loose.

I went back to Munich. A few days later my mother was discharged from hospital. My sister looked after her with the help of a visiting carer. I phoned my sister. Our mother was better, she could already move the fingers of her hand a little. Wait a moment. I heard a rustling sound and then a babble. It hurt every time, much worse than seeing her, it hurt not to hear that familiar bright voice, that laughter usually ending in an *Oh no!* She couldn't laugh any more. I understood nothing she said. When I was with her, communication had still been possible in spite of her condition, through familiar gestures, mimicry, above all through the memories from childhood that brought me so close to her, the pressure of her hands, our Morse code.

A month later I visited her at home. She was in her bed, where I had slept when I came to visit her in the past. She used to move into the living room and sleep on a folding bed. I would rather have slept in that folding bed myself, and would probably have slept better there, since it had no head and foot boards. But she insisted on sleeping in it, and always neatly made up her own ivory-white bedstead for me with fresh bedclothes, an especially soft under-blanket, a pillow at the head and another at the foot to pad the footboard. The downy feathers in the duvet collected at the foot end overnight as if in a sack, leaving the cover empty at the top.

This time she occupied her own bed and I slept in the folding bed. My sister had ironed a shirt for me, white with two breast pockets and horn buttons, a shirt from America which she, my mother, had often ironed when I came to visit, saying it was a shirt like a sail, the cotton was so firmly woven. My sister had hung the shirt in the cupboard opposite the bed.

My mother looked from her bed to the shirt and murmured something that I understood only after asking her several times: *I like that shirt.*

Only later did I realise that she probably wanted it for her shroud.

Shortly afterwards she had a second stroke and was taken back to hospital. Next morning, very early, the ward sister phoned and said my mother was very ill.

I drove to the airport, flew to Hamburg, took a taxi. Warm wind blew in through the open window, the air smelled of dry leaves and the stagnant water in the canals.

My sister came to meet me in the hospital corridor, and said our mother had died two hours earlier.

She was lying in a small room, little more than a cupboard, with just enough space for the bed and a chair. There she lay, and the surprising thing was that she was even smaller, even more fragile, this woman of such strong will, such great tenacity, who nevertheless didn't want to dominate anyone. Covered with a white blanket, her hands lying upon it loosely clasped, not folded – she had left the Church. The nurses had put daisies on the pillow and the blanket around her; they grew in the front garden of the hospital. Hands like a child's. Although she was nearly ninety they had no age spots. I carefully took her right hand. It was a shock to feel it so cold. Gently, I raised one finger, and for a moment I felt she was smiling. Her cheeks were cold too, slightly lifted by a strip of fabric tied around her chin. Only behind her head, at the back of her neck, did I still feel a little of her living warmth.

Cars driving by, voices in the corridor, a blackbird singing outside the open window. We used to call blackbirds Otto in the old days, when she and I had our secret code for them and so many other things; no one knew who we meant by Daddum's rice dwarf. A shared treasury of language. For a while we had a world that only we knew, in which we moved like conspirators, she and I, we knew it wasn't just the new names we gave things, they referred to some particular situation we had experienced together. This too was part of the sense of protection, an utterly reliable kind of protection, never in any question.

I went out into the sunlight, into that hot summer's day, I walked along the Isebek canal, the water was grey-green, the sun looked black in it, but that was only the shadow of the bridge. The wind had died down, and there was a great stillness in the sky.

She had wanted to see his grave, the place where he was buried. Snamyenka. We even knew the number of the grave, *Hero's Grave L 302*, precisely recorded in the letter from the SS doctor. She always wanted to be able to stand beside it once, or at least somewhere near it, because she knew the Russians had levelled out the war graves. After the war the Soviet government even sited rubbish dumps or factories on German military cemeteries. Nothing was to be left as a reminder of the fallen invaders.

It was my mother's enduring wish to be physically close to him if she could, just once, to say goodbye. Travelling there on her own was out of the question at the time.

No permits were given for private visits to the Soviet Union. She was already seventy-four when she went on the bus trip to Poland, the Soviet Union, Finland and Sweden. They travelled by way of Minsk.

She hoped to hire a Russian private car for an excursion at the closest point on the tour to Snamyenka. She did not underestimate the distance and the conditions, but she wanted to try, although it is likely even she doubted she would succeed.

I have her drawings and photographs from this trip, snapshots showing nothing special, but they must have meant something to her. Roads, peasant cottages as well as new buildings, tractors, passers-by.

A travelling companion, an elderly woman, kept a diary of this trip which precisely recorded places and times, and later she carefully typed it all out, with a copy for my mother.

7 June (Whit Monday)
12 noon
Not very far from Minsk we stopped outside a huge memorial site and got out. A gigantic mound rose before us, 'The Hill of Fame' it was called, made of blood-soaked earth from the last war. The place impressed me a great deal. A different kind of memorial site, without monuments.
1 p.m.
The bus went from village to village over an endless distance. I thought of the Second World War, in my mind I can hear the Wehrmacht report and see the German soldiers marching through the Russian steppes and swamps. What a time – it makes you feel melancholy. About 200 km beyond Minsk there are apple

and cherry trees still in blossom. The Russian spring is beaut-
iful – but late.

When my mother died she bequeathed to me her wish to go there. She hadn't asked me to go, yet I felt it like a pressing need, a duty, although I had never made her any promise. I wanted to write about him, but I had never thought of going to Ukraine to see the place where he lay buried. I can't even say exactly when the idea slowly became a plan, but at any rate not until after her death. Probably when I began seriously studying his diary and letters, and thought that at some point I must see the landscape where he had fought, where he was wounded and fell. Where he had wounded and killed other men.

4 August
Back to Belgorod again. Wehrmacht can't hold it. Ivan broken through.

5 August
Russ. aircraft attack km-long column. Petrol-driven vehicles blow up. 2 dead and 3 wnded in Comp.

6 August
Still moving on.

This is his last dated entry. *Still moving on.*
    After that comes one more entry, undated, a note made some time between 7 August and the day he was wounded, 19 September 1943, written carefully in rounder

handwriting and with a more distinct pressure of the pencil: *I close my diary here, because I don't see any point in recording the cruel things that sometimes happen.*

Writing about suffering, about the victims, should also mean asking questions about the killers, about guilt, about the reasons for cruelty and death – like the idea of the recording angels who keep the books, writing down all the shameful deeds and suffering of mankind.

That at least one should do – bear witness.

I had written to the military history archives in Freiburg and asked to see the war logbook of the Death's Head Division for 1943. When I arrived I found the file empty. Its contents were missing, and the archivist couldn't tell me where they had gone. Perhaps the records had been left in the USA, where these files had been taken after the war.

Why?

I was invited to give a reading in Kiev, and planned to drive on afterwards by car to Snamyenka, almost eight hundred kilometres away. Iris Klose of the German Book Trade Association, who was working for the German Book Fair in Kiev, had found me an interpreter and a man with a car who would drive us. On the day after my arrival, which happened to be the time of year when my brother had been wounded, I was woken in my hotel in the morning by the telephone. I had been dreaming, a dark dream which became even more obscure as I woke with a start, but he had figured in it, in a shadowy way. Alarmed,

I tried to stand up. I couldn't. I felt intolerable pain in both legs. I rolled out of bed, crawled across the floor towards the ringing phone, bumping into the table and chairs in the darkened room. When I lifted the receiver there was a voice, indistinct and far away, and after I said Hello several times it suddenly fell silent.

Sitting in an armchair, I gradually woke up properly and managed to locate the pain in my calves: cramp in both legs, a cramp which slowly ebbed only when I pressed my feet down on the floor. I stood up, shaved, showered, dressed. The driver who was to take me to the university was already waiting down in reception.

The discussion with the Ukrainian academics and teachers of German was very cordial, shaming us if we think of the past. The ravine of Babi Yar is near Kiev.

In the coffee break I went to the lavatory. Looking in the mirror, I saw someone else. A pale face, almost white, the eye sockets deeply shadowed and violet, like those of a dying man.

Later I asked the woman who had chaired the discussion if she had noticed the change in my eyes while we were all talking.

Yes, she said, but she hadn't wanted to say so, she thought I wouldn't like her to mention it, but suddenly, in the middle of the discussion, this dark discolouration had spread under both eyes as if I had been punched there.

That afternoon I rang the representative of the German War Graves organisation at the German Embassy and asked about the Snamyenka cemetery. It had been dug up a few weeks earlier, I was told, and there were now seven thousand skeletons lying in an empty factory building. But the man with the key to it wasn't there, he had gone to the Crimea to prepare for their reburial. There's not much to see, said the man at the Embassy. Part of the former cemetery had already had a factory built over it. He asked me the number of the grave, but as the cemetery had just been dug up that got us no further. When he heard that my brother's legs had been amputated he asked which leg had been amputated at what height. Was that important for the identification of other skeletons?

Yes. But you can't get into the factory, it's locked up.

For a moment I hesitated, wondering whether to cancel the car. But then I went after all, I went to the Dnieper, the place where the Red Army had crossed the river, in a fierce battle that cost the lives of a hundred thousand Russian soldiers. Balyko-Shchuchinka. A large, ugly monument stands there with the names of all the Soviet regiments that took part in the battle. It is up on a hill, and there is a sweeping view over the Dnieper, which is now dammed, to the flat land stretching east. Clouds piled high drifted slowly above the river, shining white.

We sat in the grass, and the driver unpacked the cans of caviar we had bought for a few dollars in a market in Kiev. He had forgotten to bring a can opener, so he opened them with his penknife, carefully bending back the jagged metal edges. We scooped the caviar out with white plastic spoons and drank vodka from water glasses. A woman came by with a basket and gave us hardboiled eggs and pickled tomatoes. We offered her some of the caviar, but it was vodka she really wanted.

Then we drove on to Kanim, a town on the Dnieper. This journey took me as close as I would get to the site of my brother's grave. The town had been rebuilt after the damage it had sustained during the war. Grey, slab-like buildings, uniformly ugly. A bus station with sunken paving, a low shelter for protection from the weather, and opposite it a building which I took to be a factory. In fact it was the theatre, but there had been no performances there for years. The one major industry in the town, an electricity plant, had been closed down. Unemployment was ninety per cent.

The Ukrainian driver, who spoke very good German, suggested we should visit his parents. Their dacha lay on a hill outside the town. Next to the little wooden house stood the structure of a larger, detached house which the driver's father had been building for years. He was a man in his late fifties, his hair dyed such a deep black that it shone like coal in the afternoon sun.

He showed us the shell of the house which he had put up himself, with only occasional help from his son. We walked on planks over the concrete that was to be a patio one day. Iron bars on the walls to right and left. There was a small concrete mixer covered with plastic, heaps of sand, bricks, buckets. This was where the walls for the second storey would go up the following year; it will take time, said the son, we have to get hold of all these things first, the iron and concrete.

Can't you buy the cement and the iron?

He laughed. No. Only organise them.

Other self-built houses stood on the slope in an anarchic variety of shapes, the result of whatever their builders had been able to organise. Chickens and ducks ran around in the gardens, a pig was poking about in the leaves. We sat in the garden outside the wooden house, drinking coffee. Later the driver's father fetched a bottle of vodka, and his mother brought out anchovies and pickled eggs.

I asked the son to ask his father, who was a little older than me, whether he could remember the war.

He shook his head without looking at me. I could see he didn't want to talk about it. After a brief moment he turned to me and raised his glass. We drank to each other. *Drushba!*

I spent that afternoon sitting in the garden outside the half-finished building, thinking that it was better to sit here with these people than to drive on.

Kruse was a furrier's apprentice in the firm where I trained. He laughed a lot, although he was the lowest-ranking trainee. Apprentices were ranked according to the kinds of furs they were allowed to work on, and that in turn depended on their craftsmanship and skill. A master furrier whose name was also Kruse, Walter Kruse, was head of this hierarchy; it consisted of twelve furriers and six apprentices. Walter Kruse made up ocelot and chinchilla, the most expensive furs. After him came two masters who made beaver and nutria coats, then the trainees who made mink into coats and stoles, then those who made Persian lamb coats, a distinction being drawn between the grey natural Persian lamb and the skins dyed black, and last of all were the coats made from left-over pieces of Persian lamb. This work was done by the apprentices in their second year of training, and by Arthur Kruse. It was a tedious and fiddly job which left plenty of time for talking, since the work did not call for calculations or great skill, unlike cutting mink skins into strips and letting them out. Arthur Kruse, for whom I had to sort pieces of Persian lamb for a month during my apprenticeship, often talked about the war, and so indeed did all the other trainees and masters who had served as NCOs or lieutenants.

Arthur Kruse, who had never left Hamburg before the war, had served in Poland, Russia, the Ukraine. I have forgotten his stories of events major and minor except for one. Although Kruse was an unassuming character, and always friendly to us apprentices, this story made him a sinister figure to me for ever.

He once had to take two captured Russians from the front to an assembly point. It was the summer of 1943, a hot July day. Twelve kilometres of sandy road to get them there, twelve kilometres to walk back. After an hour he told them: *Stoi.* They looked at him as he drank from his canteen. Of course the two Russians were thirsty too, judging by the way they stared at him, and so he put the canteen down on the ground, propped it against a stone to keep it from falling over, took three or four steps back and then gestured to them to drink, keeping his rifle under his arm and his finger on the trigger.

The two of them had hesitated, but now they walked over, picked up the canteen, each took only a couple of sips, no more, and put the canteen back beside the stone.

Kruse said he had gestured to them to run for it.

The two Russians had hesitated. Go on, off you go. He had waved his hand, and then, after a moment, the two men did run. He raised his rifle and shot twice, in quick succession. I was a good shot, quick on the trigger, he said. They'd have starved to death in the POW camp anyway.

He then turned and walked back, even stopped to rest on the way, sat down, ate some bread and a piece of sausage, finished the water in his canteen. Then he went on again, back to his unit, and reported two prisoners shot trying to escape.

Just as well, said his sergeant.

Arthur Kruse limped. Eight shell splinters had hit him in the legs shortly before the end of hostilities.

These were the everyday stories told after the war, at work, in bars, at home, in dialect or in educated High German, and they ground down and wore away what had happened, and with it the guilt. And you could talk about it perfectly freely – something that seems unimaginable today. The Russians were still the enemy who had raped women, driven Germans out of their homes. They were still starving German prisoners of war, and no one asked questions about guilt, or the chronology and causes of these cruelties. The Germans themselves had only been carrying out orders. From the private all the way up to Field Marshal Keitel, who explained to the Nuremberg court that he was not guilty, for after all, he had been obeying orders.

An uncle who had joined the SS was briefly, for a month or so, one of the SS guards at Neuengamme concentration camp. Apparently it made him feel ill. Johann, known as Jonny, never could stand the sight of blood, said my Aunt Grete. He had volunteered to leave the guards and go to the front, and he joined the Waffen SS in Bosnia. A photograph showed him wearing a fez. After the war he spent two years in an American internment camp. This uncle did not visit our home, but we met him at large family parties. I remember his complaints of the Americans' harsh treatment of their prisoners. We had to eat grass at first, he said. He had a fine baritone voice, and sometimes sang hit songs and operetta arias. I am the Count of Luxembourg. A fervent nationalist. Once when he was on leave, my paternal grandmother, a very forthright woman who was standing on a ladder hanging up net curtains at the time, is said to have slapped his face with the curtains, washed and still wet, when he said that there was nothing wrong with what was happening to the Jews.

We didn't know.

My mother, who took no interest in politics, none the less wondered about her own guilt, not tormenting herself,

119

but thinking about it, asking herself: what could I have done, what should I have done? I should have asked questions at least, she said. Where had the two Jewish families who lived near us gone? At least we should have asked that question, and not just of ourselves, we should have asked the neighbours too, in fact everyone. You can't form any opposition to something unless it's been talked about first.

The fact that people didn't talk about it can be explained by the deeply rooted need to be inconspicuous, to be one of the *community*, fearing that their careers might be disadvantaged, that obstacles might be placed in the way of promotions, and in the background there was fear of the regime's reign of terror. Hushing it up was a kind of cowardice that became a habit.

In the early fifties, when the Federal Government decided to rearm, an aunt, my father's sister, came and asked my mother if she would go with her to a demonstration in the Rathausmarkt against rearmament. The aunt's husband, who owned a firm that cleaned tankers, wasn't to know about it.

Did my mother go with her? I neglected to ask – as I neglected so much else.

For my father the end of the war, the Nazi period that ended with unconditional surrender, was not an occasion for grief at the destruction of what he called *the* German Reich, emphasising the first word; instead, he reacted with an attitude of morose injury and opinionated carping.

While always proclaiming that he had not been a Nazi, he put forward arguments to the effect that the Allies were guilty too: why hadn't the British and Americans bombed the railway tracks leading to the concentration camps? The Allies knew about them by 1943. And why didn't they bomb the crematoria? Why hadn't the USA and England taken in the Jews in time?

An attempt to make the guilt relative, to shift our own guilt to the victors, to make them guilty too.

Even if the boy I was did not see it as clearly as that, I had this feeling – at first I could not articulate it – that these were excuses, that my father was doing just what he always condemned as contemptible – he was *shamming*, he was *ducking out of responsibility*. He wouldn't face facts. Things that the child had admired, had imitated in his games on the banks of the Elbe: Rommel in Africa, defending positions to the last man, reckless attacks on British positions (in children's games you could still win the war in retrospect), *holding out*, *standing firm*, all this was now revealed as weakness and cowardice.

Perhaps that was the deeper reason why the boy, no longer a child now, resisted his father's outrage and started writing. He did not yet formulate all this critically, but he tried to present fictional characters in situations of conflict. Hatred, indignation, contempt. Not just because of his father's petty prohibitions, his prejudices about movies, music, fashion; it was his weakness, his shilly-shallying, his perceptible avoidance of any sense of his own guilt, a guilt arising not from a single obvious transgression but from an attitude that acknowledged only

121

orders and obedience. And whom had he obeyed? Who gave the orders, how were they passed on, and what did those orders say? He would not face the responsibility. He talked his way out of it. He did what he thought contemptible in others. Once the boy had noticed this, he realised that all those men who had won decorations, Close Combat Clasps, Iron Crosses, Knight's Crosses, were talking their way out of it too, wouldn't take any responsibility. One of those exculpatory phrases: *acting under orders.*

After the war, the pretext of having acted under orders allowed mass murderers to walk free, and left the way open for them to resume their lives as judges, medical experts, police officers, university professors.

My attempt to find in my memory those moments when we felt close to each other, so that I can avoid pinning labels on him too hastily, succeeds only if I look steadily at those times when the two of us, he and I, did something together. His stories bring him close to me, his voice, a calm voice of medium register. In the evening he would tell me stories he had made up. The tale of Fat-Cheeks the inquisitive hamster who floated away on a raft to an island in the river. They were children's stories; this was directly after the war. Photos of us together show him in either uniform or suit and hat, very different from the photos of him with my brother, where he sits the little boy on his motorbike in front of him, in the car beside him, on his lap in the living room. My father was in his late twenties then. I can't remember my friends and

I ever playing football or indeed anything else with him. He was approaching fifty and had little spare time. The reconstruction of Germany was in full spate. He had the shop, he met friends and former comrades. That was the world of grown-ups.

A phrase that accompanied me through my childhood – and it must have accompanied my brother too: Pull yourself together.

Once my father and I went for a boating trip on a little dammed-up river in Sudermühlen. We punted our way along among thickets of vegetation and creepers. I was eleven. A photograph bearing the date shows us in the boat, he in a suit, I in a white jacket and white shorts. My mother will have welcomed us home when we came back from our boat journey along this little river, more of a dammed-up stream in the Lüneburger Heide, a journey on which we seemed to lose ourselves in distant lands. I clearly remember wanting to repeat this trip with him.

And my memories of happiness in his company, without any discord, include a ten-day visit to Coburg. My mother had remained at home in Hamburg; someone had to mind the shop. In Coburg we stayed at the Goldene Traube, *the best hotel in the place*. Part of the purpose of this journey, I suspect, was for him to return to this small city where, as the eldest child in his family, he had been sent from Hamburg to live with a childless aunt. My grandmother had five children. Hans went to Coburg at the age of ten, attended school there and lived with Aunt Anna and his uncle Franz Schröder, a taxidermist with his own business. Hans had to help in the workshop after school. He was obviously good at the work, because his uncle wanted him to stay, and later would have liked him to marry his only daughter, Hans's cousin. Perhaps this part of his life, those seven years that he spent in the small town, the residential seat of the duke of Saxe-Coburg-Gotha, in a bourgeois society that knew its place but thought highly of the precepts of the nobility, explains why he clung to the dream of an aristocratic way of life.

For him, this journey was the realisation of his dream. He visited Coburg at a time when he was doing well financially, when he had *made something of himself*: he could make a good impression, and he came with his son, the afterthought. He drove the big sea-green Adler down the streets, and people admired the car when it was parked. Why he didn't bring the chauffeur, who was still with us at this time, I can only guess, but it probably suited him to drive the car himself, and surely he also felt he would be overdoing it, showing off, if he had a chauffeur driving him through the streets of Coburg. Massa could be justified in connection with the shop, but not as a private chauffeur. For this was the odd thing: even though my father lived beyond his means, no one could have said he showed off.

The high and indeed exaggerated social regard in which he was held was solely due to his appearance, his manners, his good conduct, his courtesy.

He never mentioned the thing that he could have been

really proud of, the thing for which he could have won fame: his animal taxidermy; it was much in demand with museums and highly praised in professional circles.

In Coburg he met his cousin, his nieces, friends and acquaintances. He was welcomed, he was invited out by old army comrades who were now sales reps or bank clerks, or had simply *made a good match*. In this small town, once the capital of a duchy, the old soldiers and their officers belonged to different associations. Coburg still boasted Suppliers To The Court, the relics of the duchy of Saxe-Coburg-Gotha, which came to an end with the 1918 revolution. But the old social order had lived on in this little city. An uncle who lived in Coburg sang in a naval choir and had people asking whether it was proper for him, as a retired lieutenant-commander, to do so.

Our trip took us on through Franconia, to places which had meant something to my father in his youth; we climbed up to castles and searched forests for overgrown ruins which he remembered from walking there with a guitarist he once knew. We always stayed the night in hotels that were *the best in the place*, we ate in restaurants that he had also ascertained were *the best*. He talked about history. He knew a good deal about the regional history of Franconia. He was relaxed, friendly, open-handed (as indeed he always was). On this trip I first noticed how he appealed to women; he was still slim at the time, held himself very upright – *chin tucked into his collar* – and was suntanned: he went brown quickly, a deep brown which contrasted to good effect with his fair hair and blue eyes. He wore made-to-measure suits, the edgings of their sleeves could be buttoned right down, and he usually left one button open.

As far as I know he never had a mistress during his marriage, had no relationship with any other woman. But he enjoyed seeing women attracted to him. My mother didn't mind. There was an economic side to it too – many customers, especially well-to-do ladies, came to buy coats at our shop because of him.

This was the brief time – three or at the most four years – when he was the man he wanted to be.

Stalingrad, Kharkov and Kiev were place names that came up in conversation again and again. The battle of Stalingrad. The recapture of Kharkov, in which my brother took part. Kiev, where my brother and a little later my father too had been, without meeting. At the time my brother was already back in action. It was said that before withdrawing from Kiev in 1941 the Russians mined blocks of flats, whole districts of the city, with explosives. Once the Germans had moved in they blew up the buildings by remote control.

No one talked about Babi Yar, a ravine near Kiev.

Working with the Group Staff and two commando units of Police Regiment South, Special Commando 4a executed 33,771 Jews on 29 and 30 September. Money, valuables, underwear and

items of clothing were impounded. Some were given to the
NSV, the Nazionalsozialistische Volkswohlfahrt, to be passed
on to ethnic Germans, some to the provisional municipal admin-
istration for needy members of the population.
USSR report no. 106, 7 October 1941

People had to take their clothes off before they were shot. The photographs taken by a German reporter with the propaganda company – rather surprisingly, they are in colour – show items in close-up: an artificial limb, a black shoe, a white shirt, a brown coat. Footsteps in the sand. Others are of a child's shoe, a fur coat, a brown handbag, a knitted child's cap, a letter, a book, probably a note-book. A photograph of the entire scene shows thousands and thousands of these items of clothing laid out along the slopes, some of them carefully folded, some simply flung down.

In one photograph two German soldiers are searching through the bundles of clothing lying on the ground, not for valuables but for the babies whose mothers tried to hide them under the clothes before they themselves were shot.

The photographs clearly show that the sun is shining.

There were men, some men, just a few, who refused to shoot civilians. They were not shot themselves for refusing, or demoted in rank, nor were they court-martialled. A few said no, as Browning has shown in his book, but they were not (as he puts it) *ordinary men.*

He called, my brother called. His voice came from the end of the passage. A kind of corridor. I ran along the passage, which suddenly led out into the open. A garden in which several people stood around; their shadows were white, their faces black and unrecognisable, as if in a photographic negative. My brother is standing there, black-faced, his suit – or a uniform? – light-coloured. He asks me to sing, to sing him something. I sing. I am surprised to find how well, indeed how melodiously I can do it. Suddenly he throws me a pear which I fail to catch. My alarm when it falls to the ground. And then his voice speaks to me . . . Floweraid, he says.

The monastery of Lavra in Kiev stands on a slope going down to the Dnieper. It was here that Russia's conversion to Christianity began, the guide tells me. I am following him down the narrow passages, a wax candle in my hand. The passages run underground. The founding fathers lie inside their walls; in the candlelight you can just see the holy relics behind the glass panes. Four novices sit in an extended cave also lit by candlelight. They have to live and fast down here underground for a while, near the founder of the monastery and their dead brothers, before they can take their vows. The passages wind through the earth like entrails, and those buried here really are digested in order to be resurrected to eternal life, new-born, at the end of the world. The faces of the novices talking quietly to pilgrims are pale, almost white.

When my sister was in hospital for the second time, for weeks on end, desperately longing to come home again, she wondered why her life had turned out the way it had, why things were the way they were. Not that she would have said it was all our father's fault. She talked about him a great deal, far more than about our mother, even when her speech was impaired by a slight stroke. She spoke mostly about little incidents that came into her mind, and she kept shaking her head. Often, if she had difficulty finding words for what she wanted to say, she used a term I had never heard her use before, she said – with great emphasis – mark you. Mark you, as if she could bring back what was forgotten that way.

She thought about our father's life, a life that failed. She would have seen her own life as a failure too if at the age of seventy-two, and after her operation, she had not had an experience of which she spoke again and again, very tenderly: she called it the greatest happiness of her life to have met *the man*.

The man, who had been our family doctor until he retired, lived in the same street, not far away, but the style of the dwellings there was different: small villas instead of four-storey rented apartment buildings.

Now and then my sister met the doctor in the street. They greeted each other, exchanged a few words. Then, one day in spring, she happened to meet him in little Eimsbüttler Park. Her first operation was two years in the past. She met the retired doctor, and they talked to each other as usual. He must have been seventy-six at the time. She had already heard from neighbours that his wife had died a few months before. She said how sorry she was. She had known the wife, who worked in her husband's practice. They talked about the weather a little; she told him she came to this little park every afternoon and sat on a bench if the sun was shining. She noticed that he was thin and grey-faced, his trousers were unironed, his shirt open, and she saw that it was days since he had shaved. To her, a doctor was someone who commanded respect, but she spontaneously passed her hand over his cheek and said: You ought to shave.

Who for, he asked, and there was a certain bitterness in his voice.

Two days later she met him in the park again and saw that he had shaved. At first they talked of this and that, and then he said suddenly: There, feel that, and offered her his cheek.

She stroked the cheek, and it was soft and smooth.

That was how it began. She said it had been the greatest happiness in her life. She had two and a half years left to her. She bought new things to wear, shoes with medium high heels, black patent leather shoes, trousers, pullovers in bright colours, in beige and red. Red gloves. She had never worn red gloves before. They went to Sylt together. And when I see the photo of her standing there, her hair blowing in the wind, smiling boldly, she is not at all like the sister I had known up till then, and whom I had seen through my father's eyes.

I have been leafing through that little notebook so often

in the last eleven months, over and over again. A strip of the binding has worked loose from the spine. I look again at my brother's drawing of a lion. It is leaping out from behind a tree. I suspect that my father improved the sketch later, for all my brother's other drawings are naive and clumsy. This one is made lifelike by a few details picked out with a stronger pencil stroke – the joints in the forepaw, the eyes, the nose, the teeth in the open jaws. They show a precise feeling for the essentials. I am sure my father added some lines and shadings when the notebook was sent to him. He probably wanted to make this little sketch by his son come up to his own expectations and wishes, with some other potential reader in mind – I am that reader.

My brother's diary began on 14 February 1943 with the entry:

We expect action any time now. On the alert from nine-thirty.

15 February
Danger over, waiting.

16 February
The Russians are gaining more and more ground, we lie here without going into action.

And so it goes on, day after day. The background to these laconic entries is rarely made evident, casts no light on my brother, his fears, his joys, what moved him, the pain he suffered, he does not even address any physical matters, he doesn't complain, he just records. *18 March: constant bombardment by Russians 1 bomb in our quarters 3 wnded. My Fahr MG not working I take my MG 42 and fire at 40 H sustained firing.*

There is a physical trace of my brother on this page, where his fingers left black marks like dark clouds on the paper, so that the *40 H* is barely legible. What does 40 H mean? Is it an abbreviation, HOH? Or the number 400?

Order issued by Field Marshal von Reichenau, 10 October 1941:

The soldier in the east is not just fighting by the rules of war, he also represents implacable national determination, he is avenging all the bestialities inflicted on the German people and their kind. The soldier must therefore have full understanding of the necessity of harsh but just retaliation upon the inferior Jewish race.

It is my wish that they – my brother, my father – had behaved like the German officer who walked down the street in his home town in uniform together with a Jewish friend, at a time when Jews were branded by the Star of David. The officer was dishonourably discharged from the army. His case is described in Wolfram Wette's book *Die Wehrmacht*. A brave man. But his was not the kind of courage expected in Germany, where courage always had to be shown in a group, with others, and its prerequisite was obedience. Obedience was among those Prussian virtues that included the courage to inflict violence, violence against others and against yourself, *they stood firm, they overcame their baser instincts*, the courage to kill and be killed. But the courage to say no did not count, the courage to oppose, to refuse to obey orders. If only everyone had rejected the idea of forging a fine career. I think of the grotesque contempt shown to those officers and soldiers who joined the Resistance movement, and to those who deserted.

What counts is for a man to dare to be entirely himself, standing alone, one single individual alone before God, alone with that enormous effort, bearing that enormous burden of responsibility.
Søren Kierkegaard

Since I have been working on this book, reading my brother's letters and diary over and over again, as well as many files, reports and books, rereading Primo Levi, Jorge Semprun, Jean Améry, Imre Kertész, Browning's *Ordinary Men*, since I have spent day after day reading of these incomprehensible horrors I have had pain in my eyes, first in the right eye, a torn cornea, then a few weeks later in the left eye, now recurring for the fifth time, a burning, unbearable pain. My pain threshold is not particularly low, but this pain will not let me sleep, makes reading and writing impossible. It is a pain that makes not only the injured eye weep but the other eye too, and I, one of a generation to whom tears were forbidden – boys don't cry – I weep as if I had to shed all my mother's, my father's, my brother's suppressed tears, the tears of those who didn't know, who didn't want to know what they could have known, should have known. *Wissen*, to know, derives from an Old High German root, *wizzan*, to see, to look. They did not know because they would not see, they looked away. Hence the frequent excuse: we didn't know about it. They did not want to see, they looked away.

I was dreaming – I dreamed I was running through passages in a bunker. Damp dripped from the concrete ceiling, had formed oddly shaped stalagmites on the floor. Uniformed messengers came towards me, running around the stalagmites as if they were a slalom course. Doors were forced open with iron levers. My father sat in a room ventilated from outside and told me how to dive off a ten-metre board without hitting the water flat. I dived, and woke up.

The boy had arrived late and had forgotten something he was supposed to buy. I have been trying to remember this one scene in detail for weeks, but I still don't know what the forgotten item was. His father sent the boy back home, promising him a beating that evening. Three or four hours passed, and the boy could think of nothing but the coming punishment. His father came home in the evening, closed the door, took his coat off, removed the leather belt from his trousers, told the boy to bend over and struck him.

I remember my mother trying to persuade my father to stop the punishment. I remember her asking him, indeed begging him not to do it.

But he was not just punishing the boy, he was punishing her too by showing her how to put an end to forgiving and forgetting. It was the only time he beat me. It was meant to be a lesson.

That afternoon remained in my memory: the gathering dusk announcing the coming punishment, the chastisement itself. Indignation remained with me, and anger grew.

Violence was *normal*. Children were beaten everywhere, out of aggression, out of conviction, for educational purposes, at school, at home, in the street.

The boy took his scooter out on the cycle path. A cyclist came past and hit him in the face, just like that. The boy fell off his scooter.

Quite right too, said a passer-by.

Violence at school. They beat you with a stick, with a ruler on the palm of your hand. One woman teacher once pulled out a handful of the boy's hair, and when his father saw the patch on his head he went up to the school and protested. The boy was embarrassed, as if he had been telling tales at home, so after that he never mentioned corporal punishment at school. He also experienced having to learn to write as violence. It had to do with getting rapped on the head. Spelling. Getting the ABC right. It was as if the child were defending himself against this pressure to turn phonetics into signs by keeping his voice going as part of it, listening to himself read out loud, a pleasing sound — today I still hear my voice inside my head as I read and write, my head-voice. *Words, words,*

words: I hear them with pleasure. This is how writing stays connected to the body. It was − and is − self-defence.

Violence at home and in the street was licensed by the violence of the state, by political readiness to use violence. *Readiness for war.*

Historically, violence exerted to achieve political ends was regarded as legitimate, a good thing. Hence all the streets and memorials named after battles. Conclusive proof of its success as a policy was provided by Frederick the Great's wars of aggression, by Bismarck's wars of unification, the German–Danish, Austro–Prussian and Franco–Prussian wars. Revolutionary violence was also regarded as a legitimate political means to social change in the policies of the Marxist left. Lenin admired the German general staff. Obedience to the Party. The individual is nothing, the Party is all. The soldier of the Party. The General Secretary. The Central Committee. Placing oneself at the service of an idea, although that idea did not, like Nazi ideology, hold up as a goal the inequality between leader and led, but on the contrary turned against the causes of inequality, against degradation; even so the aim of achieving a classless, fraternal society embraced violence and temporary oppression.

My admiration for the communists who had been in concentration camps and formed resistance groups there, who carried on fighting, who were banned again after the war in the Federal Republic under the Adenauer government, who went underground and doggedly fought on, sticking to their purpose of achieving equality and justice – that admiration was based in part on the *old-fashioned* virtues which my father demanded: constancy, duty, courage, all of which bound those fighters together. So I joined them. When our differences grew and I left the Party, what troubled me most was the idea of letting my comrades down. Although my decision had been made with insight and conviction, and I stood by it, I still felt distressingly like a traitor.

The courage to say no, standing out on your own. *Non servo.* It is a fall from grace in religion and in every totalitarian system that is based on obedience, on obeying orders. To say no, even in the face of social and collective pressure.

I close my diary here, because I don't see any point in recording the cruel things that sometimes happen.

I have looked at this passage and reread it again and again during the writing of this book – it was like a glimmer of light shining in the darkness.

How does he come to this insight? My brother has mentioned the death of two comrades and the loss of his home. But both events lay some time in the past. Could it be that something happened later, in action, something terrible that he could not write about in his diary? Those brief notes could not convey suffering, his own or the suffering of others. There is an absence of any sympathy – even for himself. And repetition made the futility of it seem banal, too.

Does that insight, his knowledge that he cannot write

of such cruel things, extend to his enemies and victims too, to Russian soldiers and civilians? To Jews? The diary includes no anti-Semitic remarks or stereotyped phrases like those found in letters sent from the front by other soldiers: inferior humans, filth, vermin, Russian dolts. On the other hand there is no phrase betraying anything like sympathy, no hint of any criticism of the conditions of the time, nothing to make a sudden conversion plausible. His notes show neither a killer by conviction nor incipient resistance. What they seem to express – and this I find terrifying – is partial blindness: only what is *ordinary* is recorded. All the more striking are that last sentence and the lapse of time between it and the penultimate entry, *still moving on*, as well as the realisation that he can no longer write about such *cruel things*. And then there is the wish, my wish, that the lapse of time may stand for No, for the *non servo* that comes when we abjure obedience, that requires more courage than blowing breaches in trenches for tanks to move forward. That would be the courage that leads to isolation, comes close to the pride and pain of the man who stands alone.

Pain and death were regarded as the hallmarks of a heroic attitude to life: readiness to bear pain, to be prepared to die. The affirmation of pain as an affirmation of life – a life that exerts itself in venturing to oppose all that is half-hearted, narrow-minded, mediocre, comfortable.

The Japanese General Nogi received the news of his son's death with satisfaction. His heroic attitude to life, however, had already become questionable, out of tune with the times, like any display of heroic requisites: sword, riding boots, spurs, Luftwaffe daggers. There was the new Luftwaffe dagger that my father had to buy when he went on leave – another memory, this – because as he got on the train some soldier, *one of those proletarians*, slammed the door, apparently as a civil gesture but really with a view to hitting the dagger, which was bent as a result.

The surprising and I think also the fascinating thing about reading Ernst Jünger's *In Stahlgewittern* [The Storm of Steel] is that it expresses a state of mind in which *courage in the face of death, duty, sacrifice* are still absolute values, not only social guidelines but a value system in which fighting together is intended to transcend nihilism. But my father could not and would not see that this kind of courage, duty and obedience were also the values that had kept the death factories working, even if people did not know – but could have known – about them. It was a question that our fathers, in their own generation, did not ask themselves – as if their minds lacked the tools for the job – and if that question was put to them from outside they could find no answer for it, merely offering excuses.

The changes in my father. He put on weight, his face was bloated, spongy with alcohol. His upright bearing, *chin tucked into his collar*, was a thing of the past, he slumped. He wore no tie, his shirt was unbuttoned so that he could breathe.

In fact he had heart trouble, suffered from breathlessness, he smoked and drank, he did not go to bed until two or three, got up at eleven in the morning and sometimes not until twelve, emerging from the bedroom hung over, swollen, grey in the face. Very few of the women customers who used to come because of him turned up now, and those who did came only to have small alterations made.

I have looked it up in my working journal, and sure enough, the cornea of my right eye first tore when I was reading Browning's book *Ordinary Men*.

If he had survived, what would my brother have thought of that book, *Ordinary Men*? How would he now see his time in the army? Would he be a member of one of the SS veterans' associations? What would he say if he could read that sentence of his today: *75 m away Ivan smoking cigarettes, fodder for my MG?*

And what would he, my father, have said? Would he even have picked the book up?

I tried to call out to him, I had to tell him something, even in my dream I was surprised to find myself aware that I must tell him something, without knowing what. I didn't know who had told me to do it either. But it was extremely important. I went from telephone kiosk to telephone kiosk, but every display said: Out of Service. SOS Calls Only. After some hesitation I pressed the keys for an SOS call. I heard a sonorous tone and knew it was his head-voice. What a strange word: head-voice.

After breakfast on the same morning I rang the phone number in Hamburg that had been my father's half a century earlier. My mother and then my sister took it over from him: 40 50 10. A curious number, as I realized only now: added together it comes to 100 and the sum of its digits is 10. A recorded message said that the number had not been recognised.

Another thing I realised only while I was writing this book: my father never said anything about his childhood. He had a hard time, one of my aunts said, with that uncle the taxidermist in Coburg. He had gone to the uncle when he was eleven or twelve. Apparently he did well at school, where he stood out from the other pupils by speaking correct High German with a north German accent. He must have been very lonely. He spent the first part of the day at school and helped in the taxidermist's workshop in the afternoon. He had tamed a young raven that fell out of the nest, and he used to go around with the bird on his shoulder. That is the only detail about his childhood I know.

That picture: the raven, which could probably croak a couple of words, on the shoulder of the boy who was to be my father.

My mother woke me in the night, I have the scene clearly before my eyes, my mother standing beside my bed, saying: Come quick, Father's not well.

It had been an unusually hot day, 1 September 1958. Even now, at three in the morning, it was still hot and sultry. I went down to the shop where he was lying on the floor. He lay there as if felled by a blow, between the armchair and the occasional table he had saved in wartime from the burning building. The table now lay toppled against the wall. He had probably tried to cling to it, or rather support himself on it, as he fell. His left arm was outstretched, his face grey. He lay there in his dark grey suit, and although it was so hot he hadn't taken off his jacket. *One does not remove one's jacket.* The dog was running around him, whining, licking his hands and face. A few people were standing outside the open shop door in silence. He had pulled the grille across the doorway and opened the door to let a breath of air blow in. My mother told me that later; she had been woken by the people outside calling. Passers-by had seen his legs on the floor as the door stood ajar, had pushed the door further open and saw him lying there.

Later, in the ambulance, I sat at the head of the stretcher, and the ambulance man sat beside it and asked for my father's personal details: born 5 November 1899. He was entering them on a form when the dead man's arm suddenly slipped and struck the ambulance man in the back. His alarm made the ambulance man jump and let out a little shriek. I carefully raised my father's arm, which was hanging down heavily, and replaced it on his chest. The ambulance was driving without its siren going or its blue light flashing. For a moment I thought: how odd, they're in no hurry. At the same time I knew there was no need.

We got out in the forecourt of the hospital by the harbour. The ambulance man opened the back of the vehicle and left it open. I stood and waited. It was still sultry. I looked at my father on the stretcher, a shadowy figure, his arm on his chest. After a while a doctor strolled across the yard, a cigarette in his mouth, his white coat unbuttoned. He nodded to me and got into the ambulance, then threw the half-smoked cigarette out of the door, took a small torch from the pocket of his coat and shone it into my father's eyes.

He climbed out of the ambulance, gave me his hand and said: I'm very sorry.

When I asked what my father had died of, he said: We'll have to see.

For the first year or so after his death I ran the business, working with my mother and sister to pay off his debts, and I had a recurrent dream. It went like this. The bell on the shop door rings and he comes in, a tall, shadowy figure. I feel horror. He was only pretending to be dead.

The dream went away when I moved on to college in Braunschweig to study for my final school-leaving examinations.

Sometimes, very occasionally, I feel him close to me.

A photograph, its surface cracked and brown – it would have been taken in the Baltic – shows him standing outside a peasant's cottage in the snow, army cap on his head, in uniform and boots. He stands there laughing. There is a curious likeness to my son and me, at least in this small photograph and from the perspective of the camera.

I am still working – yes, working – on what he really wanted.

At the entrance to the grounds of the cathedral of St Sophia in Kiev I heard singing, a soft, melancholy speech-song of a kind I had never heard before and which attracted me strangely. As I walked on I saw the man sitting on a wall under a maple tree. One of the itinerant singers who, so I heard later, travel the country again now that the socialist system has collapsed, singing their songs of fallen heroes and unhappy love. The memory of these epic songs must have been preserved in secret during the long seventy-year interim period. The singer was accompanying himself on the kobsa, an almost round, lute-like instrument. Suddenly he fell silent. It was a silence that left one listening until, after some time, the singer's voice rose again, softly, slowly.

I stood and listened for a long time, fascinated, and my eyes and ears were opened.

The odd thing about the diary is that it ought not to exist. Men were forbidden to keep diaries, particularly in the SS. A diary could only too easily fall into enemy hands, telling them something about the morale of the troops, and it could help them to follow the movements of the writer's unit, as indeed I have been doing now at a distance of sixty years. He must have kept the diary in secret, which explains its laconic style, the hasty writing, the abbreviations, the spelling mistakes.

What makes the existence of the diary even more remarkable is that it was sent back to my mother from the official SS centre, probably as a bureaucratic reflex action: a small cardboard box containing letters, his decorations, some photos, a tube of toothpaste and a comb. A few fair hairs, all that was left of his body, are still in the comb. The toothpaste in the tube is now rock-hard.

I close my diary here, because I don't see any point in recording the cruel things that sometimes happen.

GLOSSARY OF HISTORICAL TERMS

Dolchstoss: literally, 'dagger thrust', i.e. a stab in the back. This phrase was used, in Nazi parlance, for the alleged betrayal of the German army in the First World War by Social Democrats and Jews at home.

Freikorps: under the terms of the Versailles Treaty signed in 1919, Germany was to disarm, maintaining only a small regular army. Many former soldiers and officers then joined private fighting units called *Freikorps* (Free Corps). The political stance of the *Freikorps* was nationalist and right-wing, and the units fought Russian communists and opposed Germans who tried to form socialist local governments. The *Freikorps* were supposedly dissolved in 1921, but many of the former members of such units were attracted to the National Socialist party, to which they transferred their allegiance.

Nazionalsozialistische Volkswohlfahrt: National Socialist People's Welfare, usually abbreviated to NSV, the Nazi charity organisation.

Oberbefehlshaber des Heeres: supreme commander of the army, often abbreviated to OBH, i.e. Adolf Hitler.

Rasse- und Siedlungshauptamt: Main Race and Resettlement Office, often abbreviated to RuSHA, an SS organisation which set the standards for the ideological tenets and racial purity of SS members.

Reichsführer-SS: often abbreviated to RFSS, SS Reich Leader, i.e. Heinrich Himmler.

Schutzstaffel: Defence Unit, the full name of the SS. Originally formed as Hitler's personal guard, the SS became a large military and policing organisation. Concentration camp guards were drawn from its ranks, and elite SS troops included the Reich, Leibstandarte Adolf Hitler (Adolf Hitler Bodyguard) and Totenkopf (Death's Head) divisions, all mentioned in the present book.

Sicherheitsdienst: often abbreviated to SD, the Nazi intelligence and security service, outside the uniformed SS troops. It was set up by Heinrich Himmler and headed by Reinhard Heydrich until his assassination in 1942.

Waffen SS: Armed SS, formed in 1940 from existing SS divisions (see above), including the Death's Head Division. Over the next few years its strength rapidly grew. It was the only part of the SS not to be declared a criminal organisation at the Nuremberg Trials.

Wehrmacht: the regular German army, as distinct from the SS.

A NOTE ON THE AUTHOR

Uwe Timm was born in Hamburg in 1940. He trained to be a furrier and went to college in Braunschweig. He graduated from university in 1963, and went on to study philosophy and German literature in Munich and Paris. He was awarded his doctorate in philosophy in 1971. One of Germany's greatest contemporary writers and novelists, he now works in Munich and Berlin.

A NOTE ON THE TRANSLATOR

Anthea Bell's recent translations include E.T.A. Hoffmann's *The Life and Opinions of the Tomcat Murr* (Penguin Classics, 1999), W.G. Sebald's *Austerlitz* (Hamish Hamilton, 2001), and Sigmund Freud's *The Psychopathology of Everyday Life* (Penguin, 2002). She has received a number of translation awards, including the 2002 Schlegel-Tieck award (UK), Independent Foreign Fiction Prize (UK), and the Helen and Kurt Wolff Prize (USA), all three for the translation of W.G. Sebald's *Austerlitz*; the 2003 Schlegel-Tieck award for the translation of Karen Duve's *Rain* (Bloomsbury); and the 2003 Austrian State Prize for Literary Translation.

A NOTE ON THE TYPE

The text of this book is set in Bembo. This type was first used in 1495 by the Venetian printer Aldus Manutius for Cardinal Bembo's *De Aetna*, and was cut for Manutius by Francesco Griffo. It was one of the types used by Claude Garamond (1480–1561) as a model for his Romain de L'Université, and so it was the forerunner of what became standard European type for the following two centuries. Its modern form follows the original types and was designed for Monotype in 1929.